Patricia J. Stockham
Deans Cottage
Monkton, Nr. Honiton
East Devon EX14 9QQ
Tel: 01404-44207

TASTY
CHEESE
RECIPES

13/30

Cheese is one of the truly great foods. High in protein, rich in calcium and vitamins A and D, cheese contains many of the nutrients essential for maintaining health. It is loved for its versatility and there would be few households that do not have at least one variety of cheese in the refrigerator.

This book looks at the wonderful ways in which cheese can be used to create an array of recipes including starters, main meals and desserts. In the special chapter on cheesecakes you will find ten top cheesecakes – an irresistible section for all cheesecake lovers.

CONTENTS

THE PANTRY SHELF
Unless otherwise stated, the following ingredients used in this book are:

Cream Double, suitable for whipping

Flour White flour, plain or standard

Sugar White sugar

WHAT'S IN A TABLESPOON?
NEW ZEALAND
1 tablespoon =
15 mL OR 3 teaspoons
UNITED KINGDOM
1 tablespoon =
15 mL OR 3 teaspoons
AUSTRALIA
1 tablespoon =
20 mL OR 4 teaspoons
The recipes in this book were tested in Australia where a 20 mL tablespoon is standard. All measures are level.

The tablespoon in the New Zealand and United Kingdom sets of measuring spoons is 15 mL. In many recipes this difference will not matter. For recipes using baking powder, gelatine, bicarbonate of soda, small quantities of flour and cornflour, simply add another teaspoon for each tablespoon specified.

1

STARTERS

Whether you choose the Pear and Prosciutto Salad, the Cheese and Walnut Pâté or the traditional favourite French Onion Soup you can be assured that there will be few people who will not enjoy a starter that features nutritious and tasty cheese.

Mozzarella Parcels

Mozzarella Parcels

4 spring onions
200 g/6¹/₂ oz mozzarella cheese
4 slices ham
12 sun-dried tomatoes or
4 tomatoes, sliced
24 green olives

LEMON DRESSING
1 clove garlic, crushed
2 tablespoons olive oil
1 tablespoon lemon juice
1 tablespoon chopped fresh basil
freshly ground black pepper

1   Cut green tops from spring onions and place in a bowl. Reserve bulbs for another use. Pour boiling water over tops, then drain and cut into strips. Set aside.

2   Cut mozzarella into four slices. Wrap each slice of mozzarella in a slice of ham, then tie with a spring onion strip.

3   To make dressing, place garlic, oil, lemon juice, basil and black pepper to taste in a screwtop jar and shake well to combine. Arrange a Mozzarella Parcel, tomatoes and olives on individual serving plates or on a large platter. Drizzle with dressing and serve immediately.

Serves 4

This antipasto-style starter is also delicious served with crusty bread as a lunch or supper dish.

Minted Snow Pea Boats

18 snow peas (mangetout), trimmed

MINTED CREAM CHEESE FILLING
125 g/4 oz cream cheese
30 g/1 oz butter
4 tablespoons finely chopped fresh mint
1 teaspoon sugar
1 teaspoon horseradish relish
freshly ground black pepper

1   Drop snow peas (mangetout) into a saucepan of boiling water and cook for 1 minute. Drain and refresh under cold running water. Drain again, pat dry with absorbent kitchen paper and set aside.

2   To make filling, place cream cheese and butter in a bowl and beat until smooth. Stir in mint, sugar, horseradish relish and black pepper to taste.

3   Using a small sharp knife, split snow peas (mangetout) along one edge and spoon or pipe cheese mixture into snow peas (mangetout). Refrigerate for 30 minutes or until filling is firm.

Serves 6

To prepare snow peas (mangetout) for cooking, top and tail using a small sharp knife and pull away strings from older, larger peas. Snow peas can be steamed, boiled, microwaved or stir-fried.

SPIKED CHEESE BALLS

2 tablespoons vodka
3 slices stale rye or brown
bread, crumbed
125 g/4 oz blue cheese
125 g/4 oz cream cheese
60 g/2 oz butter, softened
1 tablespoon caraway seeds
30 g/1 oz almonds, toasted and
coarsely ground

These delicious morsels are
easy to make and will keep in
an airtight container in the
refrigerator for up to one
week. They are a great gift
for cheese-lovers.

1   Place vodka and 2 tablespoons
breadcrumbs in a bowl and set aside to
stand for 5 minutes.

2   Place blue cheese, cream cheese and
butter in a food processor or blender and
process to combine. Transfer cheese
mixture to a bowl, add breadcrumb
mixture and mix to combine. Cover and
chill for 30 minutes or until mixture is
firm enough to handle.

3   Place caraway seeds and remaining
breadcrumbs in a bowl. Place almonds in
a separate bowl. Take about 2 teaspoons
cheese mixture and roll into a ball.
Repeat with remaining mixture to make
about 60 balls. Roll half the cheese balls
in the breadcrumb mixture and half in
the almonds. Place cheese balls on a plate
lined with plastic food wrap and chill
until firm.

Makes 60

Olive Cheese Balls

125 g/4 oz grated tasty cheese (mature
Cheddar), at room temperature
45 g/1^1/$_2$ oz butter, softened
^{1}/$_2$ cup/60 g/2 oz flour
^{1}/$_2$ teaspoon cayenne pepper
25-30 pitted or stuffed olives

1   Place cheese and butter in a bowl
and beat until creamy. Sift in flour and
cayenne pepper and knead to make a
firm dough.

2   Wrap a teaspoon of dough around
each olive and place on a lightly greased
baking tray. Bake for 15 minutes or until
golden. Remove balls from tray and cool
on a wire rack.

Makes 25-30

Oven temperature
200°C, 400°F, Gas 6

These unusual cheese balls
are great to serve with drinks
or as an interesting addition
to a cheeseboard. They will
keep in an airtight container
for up to one week.

Cheese and Walnut Pate

125 g/4 oz butter, at room temperature
375 g/12 oz tasty cheese (mature
Cheddar), grated
^{1}/$_2$ cup/125 mL/4 fl oz beer
^{1}/$_2$ teaspoon Dijon mustard
1 teaspoon Worcestershire sauce
freshly ground black pepper
100 g/3^1/$_2$ oz walnut halves

1   Place butter in a bowl and beat until
light and fluffy. Mix cheese and beer,
alternately, into butter and beat until well
combined.

2   Stir in mustard, Worcestershire sauce
and black pepper to taste.

3   Line a small dish with plastic food
wrap, so that the wrap comes up the sides
of the container and hangs over the sides.
Place half the walnuts in base of container
or ramekin. Cover with half the cheese
mixture, then top with remaining walnuts
and cheese mixture. Smooth top of
cheese, cover and refrigerate for 24 hours.
To serve, turn onto a serving plate and
remove plastic food wrap.

Makes 500 g/1 lb

This pâté will keep, covered,
in the refrigerator for up to 10
days and so is great for
entertaining as you can
make it days in advance.
Rather than make one big
pâté you might like to make
individual ones for an
elegant starter. Simply divide
the mixture between
individual ramekins and serve
with a selection of crackers
and fresh or dried fruit.

*From left: Spiked Cheese Balls,
Olive Cheese Balls, Cheese and
Walnut Pâté*

BAKED GOAT'S CHEESE

For a starter with a difference serve Baked Goat's Cheese with thin slices of toast and a salad of watercress and red pepper strips. You might like to try olive and onion bread or caraway seed bread to add a special touch.

^{1}/2 cup/125 g/4 fl oz olive oil
1 tablespoon chopped fresh thyme
or 1 teaspoon dried thyme
1 clove garlic, crushed
freshly ground black pepper
440 g/14 oz goat's cheese, cut
into 4 slices
1 cup/125 g/4 oz dried breadcrumbs

1 Place oil, thyme, garlic and black pepper to taste in a shallow glass or ceramic dish and mix to combine. Add cheese slices, cover and set aside to marinate at room temperature for at least 30 minutes.

2 Drain cheese and roll in breadcrumbs to coat. Place cheese in a lightly greased baking dish and bake for 10 minutes or until golden. Serve immediately.

Serves 4

MOZZARELLA SALAD

Mozzarella is an unripened drawn curd cheese which means that it is kneaded and stretched during the manufacturing process. It is this process that gives it its soft plastic-like texture. This cheese comes in a variety of shapes and has a mild, delicate, creamy and almost sweet flavour.

2 large tomatoes, sliced
200 g/6^1/2 oz mozzarella cheese, sliced

BASIL DRESSING
^{1}/4 cup/60 mL/2 fl oz olive oil
^{1}/4 cup/60 mL/2 fl oz red wine vinegar
2 teaspoons chopped fresh basil
1 tablespoon cream (double)
freshly ground black pepper

1 Arrange tomato slices and cheese on individual serving plates or a large serving platter.

2 Place oil, vinegar, basil, cream and black pepper to taste in a screwtop jar and shake well to combine. Drizzle over salad and serve immediately.

Serves 4

'Goat's cheeses are often called chèvres which comes from the French word chèvre meaning a female goat. These cheeses are delicious with fresh fruit and a glass of dry, fruity wine.'

Baked Goat's Cheese,
Mozzarella Salad

CHEESE CIGARS

12 slices white sandwich bread,
crusts removed
2 teaspoons prepared hot
English mustard
4 tablespoons finely grated fresh
Parmesan cheese
60 g/2 oz grated mozzarella cheese
1 tablespoon snipped fresh chives
cayenne pepper
1 egg, lightly beaten
vegetable oil for deep-frying

CORIANDER PESTO
3 large bunches/300 g/9^1/$_2$ oz
fresh coriander
2 cloves garlic, crushed
60 g/2 oz pine nuts
^{1}/$_2$ cup/125 mL/4 fl oz olive oil
60 g/2 oz grated fresh Parmesan cheese
freshly ground black pepper

A pesto made with coriander
is perfect with these tasty
Cheese Cigars – serve them
as an indulgent pre-dinner
treat or snack. They are ideal
for entertaining as they need
to be refrigerated before
cooking.

1 Roll each slice of bread with a rolling
pin to flatten as much as possible.

2 Place mustard, Parmesan cheese,
mozzarella cheese, chives and cayenne
pepper to taste in a bowl and mix well to
combine. Divide cheese mixture between
bread slices and spread over half of each
bread slice. Brush unspread half of bread
slices with egg. Roll each slice up tightly
using the egg to seal rolls. Arrange rolls
side by side on a tray lined with plastic
food wrap, cover and refrigerate for 15
minutes or until ready to cook.

3 To make pesto, place coriander leaves,
garlic and pine nuts in a food processor or
blender and process until finely chopped.
With machine running, slowly pour in oil
and process mixture until smooth. Add
Parmesan cheese and black pepper to
taste and process to combine.

4 Heat 2.5 cm/1 in oil in a large frying
pan. When hot, cook cigars a few at a
time until evenly golden all over. Drain
on absorbent kitchen paper. Serve cigars
immediately with pesto.

Makes 12

Cheese Cigars

French Onion Soup

FRENCH ONION SOUP

60 g/2 oz butter
4 onions, thinly sliced
2 teaspoons flour
4 cups/1 litre/1³/4 pt chicken stock
¹/2 cup/125 mL/4 fl oz white wine
8 slices French bread, toasted
60 g/2 oz grated tasty cheese
(mature Cheddar)

1   Melt butter in a large saucepan, add onions and cook over a low heat, stirring constantly, for 10-15 minutes or until onions are golden. Stir in flour and cook, stirring, for 5 minutes longer.

2   Increase heat to medium, stir in stock and wine and bring to the boil then reduce heat and simmer for 10 minutes.

3   Top toasted bread with cheese and cook under a preheated grill for 2-3 minutes or until cheese melts. Place cheese toasts in the base of a large soup tureen and pour over soup. Serve immediately.

Serves 4

An alternative serving suggestion is to place two cheese toasts in each soup bowl then pour over the soup.

PIQUANT SALMON ROLLS

8 slices smoked salmon
8 thin slices brown bread
butter for spreading
8 thin slices cucumber
1 teaspoon lemon juice
freshly ground black pepper
fresh dill sprigs

CREAM CHEESE FILLING
60 g/2 oz cream cheese, softened
30 g/1 oz walnuts, chopped
1 tablespoon snipped fresh chives
1 stalk celery, finely chopped
1 teaspoon lemon juice
1/4 teaspoon ground coriander
cayenne pepper

The salmon rolls can be prepared several hours in advance and kept in the refrigerator until required. The toast bases, however, are nicer eaten freshly made and the final assembly should be done just prior to serving.

1   To make filling, place cream cheese, walnuts, chives, celery, lemon juice, coriander and cayenne pepper to taste in a bowl and mix well to combine.

2   Divide filling between salmon slices and spread over each slice. Roll up to form neat rolls.

3   Lightly toast bread and using a 7 cm/3 in biscuit cutter cut out eight rounds. Lightly spread one side of each round with butter, then top with a cucumber slice and a salmon roll. Drizzle with remaining lemon juice, season to taste with black pepper and garnish with dill sprigs. Serve immediately.

Makes 8

PEAR AND PROSCIUTTO SALAD

3 pears, peeled, cored and quartered
2 tablespoons lemon juice
12 slices prosciutto or lean ham
100 g/3¹/2 oz mozzarella cheese
freshly ground black pepper
2 tablespoons olive oil
sprigs flat-leaved parsley

1   Brush each pear quarter with lemon juice and wrap in a slice of prosciutto or ham. Using a vegetable peeler, peel off slivers of mozzarella cheese.

2   Arrange three prosciutto- or ham-wrapped pear quarters and some cheese slivers on each serving plate. Season to taste with black pepper, drizzle with oil and garnish with parsley sprigs. Serve immediately.

Serves 4

This salad is also delicious made with apples or nashi pears in place of the pears.

MAIN MEALS

Cheese is the perfect basis for any main meal. As a protein food it can be served in place of, or in conjunction with, other protein foods such as grains, legumes, meat, chicken and seafood. It is an excellent source of protein for lacto-ovo vegetarians. Those worried about the fat content of traditional cheese should look for some of the newer reduced-fat and low-fat cheeses.

*Spinach and Cheese Pie,
Ricotta and Olive Pie*

SPINACH AND CHEESE PIE

10 sheets filo pastry
2 tablespoons olive oil

SPINACH AND CHEESE FILLING
1 bunch/500 g/1 lb spinach, stalks
removed and leaves finely shredded
1 tablespoon olive oil
1 onion, finely chopped
200 g/6^1/$_2$ oz ricotta cheese
200 g/6^1/$_2$ oz feta cheese, mashed
2 tablespoons grated Parmesan cheese
4 eggs
pinch ground nutmeg
freshly ground black pepper

1 To make filling, boil, steam or
microwave spinach until just tender.
Drain and cool completely, then squeeze
to remove excess liquid. Place spinach in
a bowl.

2 Heat oil in a frying pan, add onion and
cook for 4-5 minutes or until golden. Add
to bowl with spinach and mix to combine.
Add ricotta, feta and Parmesan cheeses to
spinach mixture. Place eggs, nutmeg and
black pepper to taste in a bowl and whisk
to combine. Mix egg mixture into spinach
mixture.

3 Layer 5 sheets of pastry together,
brushing between each sheet with a little
oil. Repeat with remaining sheets. Line a
deep-sided, lightly greased ovenproof dish
with a pastry layer. Trim edges with
scissors leaving about 2.5 cm/1 in hanging
over edge of dish. Spoon in filling and top
with remaining pastry layer. Carefully fold
edges of pastry together and brush top of
pie with oil. Bake for 40-45 minutes or
until golden and crisp.

Serves 8

Oven temperature
200°C, 400°F, Gas 6

To reduce the amount of oil
required when using filo
pastry simply brush every
second or third sheet of
pastry with oil. The finished
result will be lower in kilojoules
(calories) and you will not
notice any difference in
taste.

RICOTTA AND OLIVE PIE

250 g/ 8 oz prepared shortcrust pastry

RICOTTA AND OLIVE FILLING
200 g/6^1/$_2$ oz ricotta cheese
90 g/3 oz grated Parmesan cheese
^{1}/$_2$ cup/30 g/1 oz breadcrumbs, made
from stale bread
3 eggs, lightly beaten
^{1}/$_2$ cup/125 mL/4 fl oz cream (double)
freshly ground black pepper
100 g/3^1/$_2$ oz green stuffed olives, sliced

1 Roll out pastry and line the base and
sides of a lightly greased 23 cm/9 in flan
tin. Line pastry case with nonstick baking
paper, fill with uncooked rice and bake for
15 minutes. Remove paper and rice and
bake for 10 minutes longer or until pastry
is golden. Set aside to cool slightly.

2 To make filling, place ricotta and
Parmesan cheeses, breadcrumbs, eggs,
cream and black pepper to taste in a bowl
and mix to combine. Stir in three-quarters
of the olives. Spoon filling into pastry case
and top with remaining olives. Bake for
35-40 minutes or until filling is set. Stand
for 10 minutes before serving.

Serves 6

Oven temperature
180°C, 350°F, Gas 4

Ricotta cheese is considered
to be one of the great
cooking cheeses. It is a soft,
white cheese with a creamy
texture and a sweetish
flavour. As it is an unripened
cheese it does not keep well
and should be eaten within
2-3 days of purchase. Any
yellowing of the cheese
indicates that it is old.

BLUE CHEESE QUICHE

Oven temperature
180°C, 350°F, Gas 4

200 g/6¹/2 oz prepared shortcrust pastry

BLUE CHEESE FILLING
30 g/1 oz butter
3 onions, thinly sliced
2 cloves garlic, crushed
3 eggs, lightly beaten
60 g/2 oz blue cheese, mashed
1 cup/250 mL/8 fl oz milk
³/4 cup/185 g/6 oz sour cream
2 teaspoons caraway seeds
freshly ground black pepper

1   Roll out pastry and line the base and sides of a lightly greased 23 cm/9 in flan tin. Line pastry case with nonstick baking paper, fill with uncooked rice and bake for 15 minutes. Remove paper and rice and bake for 10 minutes longer or until pastry is golden. Set aside to cool slightly.

2   To make filling, melt butter in a frying pan, add onions and garlic and cook over a low heat, stirring constantly, for 10 minutes or until onions are golden. Spoon onion mixture over base of pastry case.

This delightful quiche becomes a complete meal when served with a tossed green salad and wholemeal rolls. Delicious hot or cold, it is also ideal for picnics and lunch boxes.

3   Place eggs, blue cheese, milk, sour cream, caraway seeds and black pepper to taste in a bowl and mix to combine. Carefully pour egg mixture over onion mixture. Bake for 30 minutes or until quiche is set and lightly browned.

Serves 4

MOZZARELLA-TOPPED VEAL

30 g/1 oz butter
4 veal schnitzels (escalopes)
$^1/4$ cup/60 mL/2 fl oz dry white wine
440 g/14 oz canned tomatoes, undrained and mashed
1 teaspoon chopped fresh basil
freshly ground black pepper
125 g/4 oz grated mozzarella cheese

1   Melt butter in a large frying pan, add veal schnitzels and cook for 1 minute each side. Remove veal from pan, place in a shallow baking dish, set aside and keep warm.

2   Add wine to pan and bring to the boil, reduce heat and simmer until reduced by half. Stir in tomatoes and basil and simmer for 10 minutes. Season to taste with black pepper.

3   Spoon tomato sauce over veal and sprinkle with mozzarella cheese. Bake for 10 minutes or until cheese melts. Serve immediately.

Serves 4

Oven temperature
200°C, 400°F, Gas 6

This easy veal dish combines the best of Italian flavours. It is also delicious made with pork, chicken or turkey schnitzels (escalopes). Serve with a green salad of mixed lettuces and herbs tossed in a garlicky dressing.

15

RISOTTO PRIMAVERA

375 g/12 oz yellow baby squash,
cut into quarters or 2 carrots, sliced
4 zucchini (courgettes), sliced
250 g/8 oz asparagus spears, cut into
2.5 cm/1 in pieces
2 red peppers, cut into quarters
freshly ground black pepper
3 tablespoons grated Parmesan cheese

RISOTTO
125 g/4 oz butter
2 leeks, sliced
2 cloves garlic, crushed
500 g/1 lb Arborio or risotto rice
1 cup/250 mL/8 fl oz dry white wine
1/4 cup/60 mL/2 fl oz tarragon vinegar
2 bay leaves
3 cups/750 mL/1 1/4 pt chicken or
vegetable stock
6 sun-dried tomatoes, chopped or
2 tomatoes, peeled and chopped
1 tablespoon chopped fresh basil

1 To make Risotto, melt butter in a heavy-based saucepan, add leeks and garlic and cook over a medium heat for 5 minutes or until leeks are soft. Stir in rice, tossing well to coat with butter.

2 Stir in wine and vinegar, bring to simmering and simmer until most of the liquid is absorbed. Add bay leaves and 2 cups/500 mL/16 fl oz stock. Simmer until liquid is absorbed. Stir in tomatoes and remaining stock and simmer, stirring frequently, until liquid is absorbed and rice is tender. Stir in basil and black pepper to taste.

3 Boil, steam or microwave squash, zucchini (courgettes) and asparagus separately until tender. Set aside and keep warm. Grill red peppers, skin side up until skin blisters. Peel and slice thickly. Toss vegetables together and season to taste with black pepper. To serve, place Risotto on a serving plate and surround with vegetables. Sprinkle with Parmesan cheese.

Serves 8

Arborio rice is an Italian short-grain rice from the Po Valley. Short-grain rice contains more starch than long- and medium-grain rice and so becomes sticky as it cooks. Arborio absorbs liquid without becoming soft and it is this special quality that makes it most suitable for risottos. Arborio rice is recognisable by the distinctive white spot on each kernel. If it is unavailable, short-grain rice can be used instead.

*'A wedge of fresh Parmesan served with ripe pears makes
a wonderful finish to any meal'*

Risotto Primavera, Cheese and Onion Pudding

CHEESE AND ONION PUDDING

30 g/1 oz butter
3 large onions, thinly sliced
¹/₂ teaspoon dried thyme
60 g/2 oz grated Parmesan cheese
60 g/2 oz grated smoked cheese
125 g/4 oz grated tasty cheese
(mature Cheddar)
1 tablespoon snipped fresh chives
8 slices wholemeal bread,
crusts removed
3 eggs
2 cups/500 mL/16 fl oz milk
freshly ground black pepper

Serves 6

1 Melt butter in a frying pan, add onions and thyme and cook over a low heat, stirring frequently, for 10-15 minutes or until onions are golden and soft.

2 Place Parmesan, smoked and tasty (mature Cheddar) cheeses and chives in a bowl and toss to combine. Place half the bread in the base of a greased baking dish, cutting slices to fit snugly, if necessary. Cover with onion mixture and sprinkle with half the cheese mixture. Repeat with remaining bread and cheese.

3 Place eggs and milk in a bowl and whisk to combine. Season to taste with black pepper. Pour egg mixture over bread and cheese in baking dish and bake for 30-35 minutes or until firm and golden.

Oven temperature
190°C, 375°F, Gas 5

This delicious savoury version of bread and butter pudding is a great way to use up day-old bread and to make the most of any oddments of cheese. You might like to try other cheeses, such as blue, Camembert or Gouda, depending upon what you have in your refrigerator.

DEEP-SIDED TUNA PIZZA

Oven temperature
220°C, 425°F, Gas 7

Pizza Dough
Use this dough for the base of the Deep-sided Tuna Pizza, the Artichoke and Salami Pizza and the Gorgonzola Pizza.
Dissolve 1 teaspoon active dry yeast and a pinch of sugar in ²/₃ cup/170 mL/ 5¹/₂ fl oz warm water in a large mixing bowl. Set aside to stand in a warm draught-free place for 5 minutes or until foamy. Place 2 cups/ 250 g/8 oz flour and ¹/₂ teaspoon salt in a food processor and pulse once or twice to sift. With machine running, slowly pour in ¹/₄ cup/60 mL/2 fl oz olive oil and yeast mixture and process to form a rough dough. Turn dough onto a lightly floured surface and knead for 5 minutes or until soft and shiny. Add more flour if necessary.
Lightly oil a large bowl, then roll dough around in it to cover the surface of the dough with oil. Cover bowl tightly with plastic food wrap and place in a warm draught-free place for 1¹/₂-2 hours or until dough has doubled in volume.
Knock down and remove dough from bowl. Knead briefly before using.

Pizza Dough (see recipe)
olive oil
440 g/14 oz canned tuna, drained, broken into chunks
lemon juice
freshly ground black pepper
375 g/12 oz grated mozzarella cheese
4 tablespoons grated Parmesan cheese
2 tablespoons chopped fresh parsley
60 g/2 oz pitted black olives
10 whole anchovy fillets, drained and halved lengthwise

TOMATO SAUCE
2 tablespoons olive oil
1 large red onion, cut into slices, lengthwise
1 green pepper, sliced
1 clove garlic, crushed
4 tomatoes, peeled, seeded and chopped
¹/₂ teaspoon sugar
1 tablespoon minced anchovy fillets
freshly ground black pepper

1   Prepare Pizza Dough. Brush a 33 cm/ 13 in pizza tray with olive oil and line with dough, pressing dough up sides to form a 4 cm/1¹/₂ in rim. Brush dough with oil and set aside.

2   To make sauce, heat oil in a large frying pan, add onion, green pepper and garlic and cook over a medium heat for 6-8 minutes or until onion is soft. Stir in tomatoes, sugar, minced anchovy fillets and black pepper to taste.

3   To assemble, place tuna, lemon juice and black pepper to taste in a bowl and mix to combine. Sprinkle one-third mozzarella cheese and 1 tablespoon Parmesan cheese over pizza dough. Top with half the tuna mixture, sprinkle with 1 tablespoon parsley and half the olives. Spoon half the sauce mixture over, then repeat layers finishing with a layer of mozzarella and remaining Parmesan cheese.

4   Fold excess dough back on itself and crimp edges neatly. Arrange anchovy fillets in a diamond pattern on top of pizza. Halve remaining olives and place one in the centre of each diamond. Drizzle over some olive oil and bake for 15-20 minutes or until golden.

Serves 6

*Deep-sided Tuna Pizza, Artichoke and
Salami Pizza, Gorgonzola Pizza*

ARTICHOKE AND SALAMI PIZZA

Pizza Dough (see recipe)
olive oil
300 g/9^1/$_2$ oz thinly sliced
mozzarella cheese
100 g/3^1/$_2$ oz thinly sliced salami
4 canned artichoke hearts, thinly
sliced lengthwise
freshly ground black pepper

1   Prepare Pizza Dough. Roll out dough
into a rectangle 1 cm/^{1}/$_2$ in thick and
press into a lightly oiled shallow 18 x 28
cm/7 x 11 in tin. Bring dough up at sides
to form a slight rim. Brush with olive oil.

2   Place slices of mozzarella, slices of
salami and slices of artichoke hearts
slightly overlapping in lines along width
of dough to cover entire surface. Sprinkle
generously with oil and season to taste
with black pepper.

3   Bake for 15 minutes, then reduce oven
temperature to 190°C/375°F/Gas 5 and
bake for 10 minutes longer or until cheese
is bubbling and crust is golden. Remove
from oven and rest briefly before serving.

Not all pizzas need a layer of
tomato sauce to give them
flavour and keep them moist.
This tasty combination of
toppings is a delicious and
striking example of just how
good a pizza without tomato
can be.

Serves 6

GORGONZOLA PIZZA

Pizza Dough (see recipe)
^{3}/$_4$ cup/185 mL/6 fl oz olive oil
1 large eggplant (aubergine), cut into
5 mm/^{1}/$_4$ in slices
155 g/5 oz Gorgonzola or
soft blue cheese
400 g/12^1/$_2$ oz ricotta cheese, drained
1 teaspoon finely chopped fresh sage or
^{1}/$_4$ teaspoon dried sage
3 tablespoons pine nuts
3 tablespoons grated Parmesan cheese
freshly ground black pepper
fresh sage leaves (optional)

1   Prepare Pizza Dough. Shape into a
38 cm/15 in circle and place on a baking
tray. Bring up sides to form a slight rim.

2   Heat ^{1}/$_2$ cup/125 mL/4 fl oz oil in a
large frying pan and cook eggplant
(aubergine) slices a few at a time until
lightly browned on both sides. Drain on
absorbent kitchen paper.

3   Place Gorgonzola, or blue cheese, and
ricotta in a bowl and mix well to
combine. Spread cheese mixture evenly
over dough. Top with eggplant
(aubergine) slices, then sprinkle with sage,
pine nuts, Parmesan cheese and black
pepper to taste. Finally drizzle with
remaining olive oil and top with fresh
sage leaves, if using.

4   Bake for 15 minutes, then reduce heat
to 190°C/375°F/Gas 5 and bake for 10
minutes longer.

This pizza is as good straight
from the oven as it is cooled
and taken on a picnic.
Shaping the dough, then
allowing it to rise a second
time, for 30 minutes, before
topping will give a thicker,
more bread-like crust.

Serves 6

Pork Chops with Cheese Crust

PORK CHOPS WITH CHEESE CRUST

60 g/2 oz grated **Parmesan cheese**
3 tablespoons **mango chutney**
1 tablespoon **Dijon mustard**
1 tablespoon **wholegrain mustard**
2 **pork chops, trimmed of all visible fat**
³/4 cup/90 g/3 oz **dried breadcrumbs**

1   Place Parmesan cheese, chutney and Dijon and wholegrain mustards in a bowl and mix to combine.

2   Spread chops generously with cheese mixture, then roll in breadcrumbs to coat. Place chops on a rack set in a baking dish and bake for 25-30 minutes or until chops are cooked.

Serves 2

Oven temperature
180°C, 350°F, Gas 4

You will find this crust just as delicious as a coating for lamb chops.

PASTA AND VEGETABLE BAKE

Oven temperature
200°C, 400°F, Gas 6

An economical dish that is
sure to become a family
favourite. You can vary it
depending on the time of
year and what vegetables
are available and liked by
your family.

250 g/8 oz pasta
shapes of your choice
1 tablespoon oil
1 onion, chopped
1 clove garlic, crushed
1 carrot, chopped
1 stalk celery, chopped
1 zucchini (courgette), chopped
1 small head broccoli, broken into
small florets
440 g/14 oz canned tomatoes, mashed
and undrained
3 tablespoons tomato paste (purée)
2 tablespoons dry white wine
freshly ground black pepper
250 g/8 oz grated mozzarella cheese

Serves 4

1   Cook pasta shapes in boiling water in
a large saucepan following packet
directions. Drain and set aside.

2   Heat oil in a frying pan, add onion,
garlic, carrot and celery and cook, stirring
occasionally, over a medium heat for 10
minutes or until vegetables are soft.

3   Add zucchini (courgette), broccoli,
tomatoes, tomato paste (purée) and wine,
and cook for 20 minutes, stirring
occasionally. Add a little water, if
necessary, to keep mixture moist. Add
pasta to vegetable mixture, season to taste
with black pepper and mix to combine.

4   Spoon vegetable mixture into a
shallow ovenproof dish, sprinkle with
cheese and bake for 10-15 minutes or
until cheese melts.

BRIE AND BACON PIE

CHEESE PASTRY
2 cups/250 g/8 oz flour
125 g/4 oz chilled butter, cut into small pieces
2 tablespoons grated Parmesan cheese
2 tablespoons iced water

BACON FILLING
125 g/4 oz bacon, chopped
1 onion, chopped
2 cloves garlic, crushed
2 tablespoons chopped fresh parsley
$^1/_2$ red pepper, chopped
4 eggs, lightly beaten
$1^1/_4$ cups/315 mL/10 fl oz cream (double)
freshly ground black pepper
200 g/6$^1/_2$ oz Brie, cut into thin slices
$^1/_4$ teaspoon ground nutmeg

1 To make pastry, place flour, butter and Parmesan cheese in a food processor and process until mixture resembles fine breadcrumbs. With machine running, slowly add water until a dough forms. Turn dough onto a floured surface and knead lightly. Wrap pastry in plastic food wrap and chill for 15 minutes. Roll out pastry on a lightly floured surface and line a greased 23 cm/9 in flan tin. Line pastry case with nonstick baking paper, fill with uncooked rice and bake for 10 minutes. Remove rice and paper and bake for 10 minutes longer.

2 To make filling, cook bacon and onion in a frying pan over a medium heat for 3-4 minutes or until onion is soft. Add garlic, parsley and red pepper and cook for 2 minutes longer. Spread bacon mixture over base of pastry case.

3 Place eggs, cream and black pepper to taste in a bowl and whisk to combine. Carefully pour egg mixture into pastry case. Arrange Brie slices on top and sprinkle with nutmeg. Reduce oven temperature to 180°C/350°F/Gas 4 and bake for 45 minutes or until pie is set.

Serves 6

Oven temperature
200°C, 400°F, Gas 6

Did you know the main difference between Brie and Camembert is the size? Traditionally a Brie is a 1 kg/ 2 lb wheel or round while a Camembert is a 125 g/4 oz round. There are also slight differences in taste and creaminess, and a ripe Brie has more moisture than a Camembert so will run more. If a recipe calls for one and it is unavailable the other can be used in its place.

Brie and Bacon Pie

LIGHT MEALS

*These meals make perfect lunch or supper dishes when served
with a tossed green salad, crusty bread and a glass of wine. They
are also quick to prepare, making them ideal for today's busy
lifestyle. So next time you are looking for something interesting
and not too heavy why not choose Grilled Goat's Cheese Salad
or Baked Camembert?*

Pizza Slice

Pizza Slice

PASTRY
1¹/4 cups/155 g/5 oz flour
1 cup/155 g/5 oz wholemeal flour
¹/2 teaspoon salt
1 teaspoon active dry yeast
2 tablespoons olive oil
³/4 cup/185 mL/6 fl oz warm water

PIZZA TOPPING
1 tablespoon olive oil
1 onion, chopped
440 g/14 oz canned tomatoes, undrained and mashed
¹/2 teaspoon dried oregano
¹/2 teaspoon dried basil
3 tablespoons tomato paste (purée)
60 g/2 oz button mushrooms, sliced
2 spring onions, chopped
125 g/4 oz ham, chopped
6 black olives, pitted and sliced
125 g/4 oz grated mozzarella cheese

1   To make pastry, place flour, wholemeal flour, salt and yeast in a food processor and process to combine. With machine running, slowly pour in oil and water and process to form a soft dough. Turn dough onto a floured surface and knead lightly.

2   Lightly oil a large bowl then roll dough around in it to cover surface of dough with oil. Cover bowl with plastic food wrap and place in a warm, draught-free place for 1¹/2-2 hours or until dough has doubled in volume. Knock down and remove dough from bowl. Knead briefly, then roll out to fit a 30 x 35 cm/12 x 14 in baking tray.

3   To make topping, heat oil in a large frying pan, add onion and cook for 5 minutes or until soft. Stir in tomatoes, oregano and basil, bring to the boil, then reduce heat and simmer, stirring occasionally, for 10 minutes or until sauce thickens and reduces slightly. Remove pan from heat and set aside to cool.

4   Spread pizza base with tomato paste (purée) then top with tomato sauce. Sprinkle with mushrooms, spring onions, ham, olives and cheese and bake for 20 minutes or until golden.

Serves 6

Oven temperature
220°C, 425°F, Gas 7

This Pizza Slice freezes well and is great to have on hand for hungry children and teenagers. A slice in a packed lunch is also sure to be popular.

'True mozzarella is made from buffalo's milk and is labelled mozzarella di bufala. It is porcelain white in colour and tastes quite different to mozzarella made from cow's milk.'

Right: Tomato and Cheese Fritters
Below: Radicchio and Pear Salad

RADICCHIO AND PEAR SALAD

1 radicchio, leaves separated
1 leek, cut into thin strips
2 pears, peeled, cored and sliced
155 g/5 oz pecorino cheese, sliced

RED VINEGAR DRESSING
1/3 cup/90 mL/3 fl oz olive oil
2 tablespoons red wine vinegar
freshly ground black pepper

Pecorino is an Italian cheese traditionally made from sheep's milk. It is similar to Parmesan cheese but has a saltier, sharper and more tangy taste. If pecorino is unavailable, Parmesan can be used in its place.

1   Arrange radicchio leaves, leek strips, pear slices and cheese slices attractively in a large salad bowl or on a large platter.

2   To make dressing, place oil, vinegar and black pepper to taste in a screwtop jar and shake well to combine. Drizzle dressing over salad and serve.

Serves 4

TOMATO AND CHEESE FRITTERS

$^1/_2$ cup/75 g/2$^1/_2$ oz oat bran
60 g/2 oz grated Swiss cheese
2 tablespoons chopped fresh basil
$^1/_2$ teaspoon caraway seeds
3 partially ripe tomatoes, cut into
thick slices
$^1/_2$ cup/60 g/2 oz flour
2 eggs, beaten
olive oil for shallow frying

1   Place bran, cheese, basil and caraway seeds in a bowl and mix to combine.

2   Coat tomato slices with flour, then dip in egg and roll in bran mixture. Place coated tomato slices on a plate lined with plastic food wrap and refrigerate for 15 minutes.

3   Heat oil in a large frying pan and cook a few tomato slices at a time for 3-4 minutes each side or until golden. Remove and drain on absorbent kitchen paper.

Serves 6

These fritters are delicious served with your favourite chutney or pickle. Serve them with a salad for a light meal, as a party snack, or as a tasty side dish at your next barbecue.

VEGETABLE AND RICOTTA CREPES

CREPES
1/4 cup/30 g/1 oz flour
3 eggs
2 zucchini (courgettes), grated
30 g/1 oz grated Parmesan cheese
1/2 cup/125 mL/4 fl oz milk
1/4 teaspoon ground nutmeg

RICOTTA FILLING
250 g/8 oz ricotta cheese
1 tablespoon lime juice
2 tablespoons snipped fresh chives
freshly ground black pepper

To keep cooked crêpes warm while making the rest of the batch, place the crêpes in a stack on a heatproof plate and place in a low oven, or over a saucepan of simmering water.

1   To make crêpes, place flour in a large bowl, make a well in the centre, add eggs, zucchini (courgettes), Parmesan cheese, milk and nutmeg. Mix well to combine.

2   Pour 2-3 tablespoons batter into a lightly greased 18 cm/7 in crêpe pan and tilt pan so batter covers base thinly and evenly. Cook over a high heat for 1 minute or until lightly browned on base. Turn crêpe and cook other side for 30 seconds. Remove from pan, set aside and keep warm. Repeat with remaining mixture.

3   To make filling, place ricotta cheese, lime juice, chives and black pepper to taste in a bowl and beat to combine. Spread 2 tablespoons of filling over each crêpe, roll up and serve immediately.

Serves 4

Left: Vegetable and Ricotta Crêpes
Below: Mozzarella and Egg Salad

MOZZARELLA AND EGG SALAD

300 g/9¹/₂ oz mozzarella cheese, cut into
2 cm/³/₄ in batons
1 bunch/250 g/8 oz watercress, broken
into small sprigs
8 hard-boiled quail's eggs, halved

CREAMY DRESSING
¹/₄ cup/60 mL/2 fl oz cream (double)
3 tablespoons mayonnaise
2 tablespoons white wine vinegar
freshly ground black pepper

1   To make dressing, place cream,
mayonnaise, vinegar and black pepper to
taste in a bowl and whisk to combine.
Add cheese batons to dressing and toss to
coat.

2   Arrange watercress sprigs on
individual serving plates or a large serving
platter. Top with cheese and quail's eggs
and serve immediately.

Serves 4

If quail's eggs are
unavailable, this salad is just
as delicious made with hen's
eggs. Use 4 hen's eggs, hard-
boiled and cut into quarters,
in place of the quail's eggs.

Right: Baked Camembert
Below: Grilled Goat's Cheese Salad

GRILLED GOAT'S CHEESE SALAD

1 radicchio, leaves separated
1 curly endive, leaves separated
440 g/14 oz canned artichoke hearts,
drained and halved
8 cherry tomatoes, halved
60 g/2 oz button mushrooms
60 g/2 oz watercress, broken into sprigs
4 x 100 g/3^1/$_2$ oz goat's cheeses
1 tablespoon olive oil

HERB DRESSING
1^1/$_2$ tablespoons lemon juice
1^1/$_2$ tablespoons cider vinegar
^{1}/$_2$ cup/125 mL/4 fl oz olive oil
1 clove garlic, crushed
1 tablespoon chopped fresh basil or
1 teaspoon dried basil
2 teaspoons chopped fresh rosemary or
^{1}/$_2$ teaspoon dried rosemary
freshly ground black pepper

1   Arrange radicchio, endive, artichokes, tomatoes, mushrooms and watercress on individual serving plates.

2   To make dressing, place lemon juice, vinegar, oil, garlic, basil, rosemary and black pepper to taste in screwtop jar and shake well to combine.

3   Brush each goat's cheese with a little oil and cook under a preheated grill for 1 minute each side or until cheese just starts to melt. Place cheese on top of salad, drizzle with dressing and serve.

Serves 4

Often known as chèvres, goat's cheeses can be eaten at different stages of ripening. A young cheese is soft and spreadable, maturing to being dry and somewhat crumbly; in fact it could be described as almost chalky.

BAKED CAMEMBERT

250 g/8 oz wheel Camembert cheese
1 egg, lightly beaten
$^{1}/_{4}$ cup/30 g/1 oz flour, sifted
155 g/5 oz shelled pistachio nuts,
chopped

RASPBERRY SAUCE
250 g/8 oz raspberries
1 tablespoon icing sugar

1 To make sauce, place raspberries and icing sugar in a food processor or blender and process until smooth. Push raspberry mixture through a sieve to remove seeds and set aside until ready to serve.

2 Dip Camembert in egg, then roll in flour, dip in egg again and finally roll in pistachio nuts to coat. Place on a baking tray lined with nonstick baking paper and bake for 10-15 minutes or until cheese softens. Serve cut into wedges accompanied by raspberry sauce.

Serves 4 as a light meal, starter or dessert

Oven temperature
220°C, 425°F, Gas 7

This versatile dish can be served with a salad and crusty bread as a light meal, or on its own as a starter, or with additional berries for dessert. Whichever way you choose to serve it you can be assured that it will be popular. For something different, you might like to use slivered almonds in place of the pistachios.

SNACKS

*Whether it's a slice of sharp Cheddar, a toasted cheese
sandwich or a cheese-flavoured quiche, cheese is one of the most
popular foods. The next time you feel like a snack to keep away
the hunger pangs you might like to choose one of the tasty
cheese recipes in this chapter.*

Mini Olive Quiches

Cheese Triangles

Cheese and Garlic
Crisps

Turkey and Stilton
Sandwiches

Peaches and Cream
Muffins

Fruit and Nut Muffins

Turkey and Cheese
Muffins

Mini Pizza Triangles

Grilled Goat's
Cheese Toast

Mini Carrot and Feta
Quiches

Blue Cheese Nibbles

*Cheese Triangles,
Mini Olive Quiches*

MINI OLIVE QUICHES

250 g/8 oz prepared puff pastry
$^1/_2$ cup/125 mL/4 fl oz milk
3 eggs, lightly beaten
$^1/_3$ cup/90 mL/3 fl oz cream (double)
30 g/1 oz grated tasty cheese
(mature Cheddar)
1 teaspoon ground paprika
freshly ground black pepper
10 green stuffed olives, sliced

Makes 4

1 Line four 7.5 cm/3 in flan tins with pastry. Line each pastry case with nonstick baking paper, fill with uncooked rice and bake for 5 minutes. Remove rice and paper and bake for 5 minutes longer.

2 Place milk, eggs, cream, cheese, paprika and black pepper to taste in a bowl and mix to combine.

3 Divide olives between pastry cases, then pour over egg mixture. Reduce oven temperature to 180°C/350°F/Gas 4 and bake for 15-20 minutes or until quiches are set.

Oven temperature
200°C, 400°F, Gas 6

Individual quiches are great to keep in the freezer to have on hand for snacks and lunch boxes. One of these quiches when frozen will take about 10 minutes to heat in an oven preheated to 200°C/400°F/Gas 6.

CHEESE TRIANGLES

2 cups/500 mL/16 fl oz milk
100 g/3$^1/_2$ oz semolina
125 g/4 oz grated tasty cheese (mature Cheddar)
2 tablespoons chopped fresh parsley
1 tablespoon snipped fresh chives
freshly ground black pepper
1 cup/125 g/4 oz dried breadcrumbs
3 tablespoons grated Parmesan cheese
1 egg, lightly beaten
vegetable oil for deep-frying

1 Place milk in a large saucepan and bring slowly to the boil. Add semolina very slowly and cook for 5 minutes, stirring constantly.

2 Remove pan from heat and stir in tasty cheese (mature Cheddar), parsley, chives and black pepper to taste. Spread

semolina mixture evenly over the base of a lightly greased, shallow 18 x 28 cm/ 7 x 11 in cake tin. Cover and refrigerate for at least 1 hour or until cold.

3 Place breadcrumbs and Parmesan cheese in a shallow dish and mix to combine. Set aside.

4 Cut the semolina mixture into triangles and dip each triangle in egg, then in breadcrumb mixture to coat.

5 Heat oil in a large frying pan until a cube of bread dropped in browns in 50 seconds. Cook triangles a few at a time for 1-2 minutes or until golden. Remove with a slotted spoon and drain on absorbent kitchen paper. Serve immediately.

Serves 4

To bring out the full flavour of cheese always allow it to come to room temperature before eating. As a general rule, remove cheese from the refrigerator 30 minutes before you intend to eat it.

CHEESE AND GARLIC CRISPS

Oven temperature
180°C, 350°F, Gas 4

The crisps will keep in an airtight container for up to a week and are great to have on hand for after-school or work snacks.

4 pitta bread rounds
125 g/4 oz butter, melted
3 cloves garlic, crushed
2 tablespoons chopped fresh basil
4 tablespoons grated Parmesan cheese

1   Split each pitta bread round in half, horizontally, then cut each half into four wedges.

2   Place butter, garlic and basil in a bowl and mix to combine. Place pitta wedges cut side up on a lightly oiled baking tray. Brush each pitta wedge with butter mixture then sprinkle with Parmesan cheese and bake for 10 minutes or until golden and crisp.

Makes 32 wedges

Left: Cheese and Garlic Crisps
Below: Turkey and Stilton Sandwiches

TURKEY AND STILTON SANDWICHES

1 French bread stick, cut into
12 thick slices
2 tablespoons Dijon mustard
12 slices smoked turkey
200 g/6$^{1}/_{2}$ oz Stilton cheese, crumbled
30 g/1 oz watercress, broken into sprigs

Spread each slice of bread with mustard. Top with turkey and cheese and garnish with watercress. Serve immediately.

Serves 6

Every country seems to have its own favourite blue cheese. Stilton is the blue cheese of Britain. For these sandwiches you can choose your favourite blue cheese. If you do not like blue cheese you might like to use Brie, Camembert or a cream cheese instead.

PEACHES AND CREAM MUFFINS

Recognised as the dieter's cheese, cottage cheese is made from skim milk and so has a fat content of only 3 per cent. Like ricotta it is one of the great cooking cheeses and is widely used in cheesecakes.

4 tablespoons cottage cheese
pulp of 1 passion fruit or 1 tablespoon
passion fruit pulp
2 muffins, split and toasted
2 peaches, stoned and sliced

Place cottage cheese and passion fruit pulp in a small bowl and mix to combine. Spread mixture over muffin halves, top with peach slices and serve immediately.

Serves 2

FRUIT AND NUT MUFFINS

Why not try these muffins as a special breakfast treat? If you do not have ricotta cheese, use cottage cheese in its place.

4 tablespoons ricotta cheese
1 tablespoon currants
1 tablespoon chopped raisins
1 teaspoon finely grated orange rind
2 muffins, split and toasted
2 tablespoons chopped pecan nuts
or walnuts

Place ricotta cheese, currants, raisins and orange rind in a small bowl and mix to combine. Spread over muffin halves and sprinkle with pecan nuts. Serve immediately.

Serves 2

TURKEY AND CHEESE MUFFINS

2 muffins, split and toasted
1 tomato, sliced
4 thin slices cooked turkey breast
3 tablespoons grated tasty cheese
(mature Cheddar)
freshly ground black pepper

Top each muffin half with tomato, turkey, cheese and black pepper to taste and cook under a preheated grill for 2-3 minutes or until cheese melts.

Serves 2

Peaches and Cream Muffins, Fruit and Nut Muffins, Turkey and Cheese Muffins

Right: Mini Pizza Triangles
Far right: Grilled Goat's
Cheese Toast

MINI PIZZA TRIANGLES

Oven temperature
180°C, 350°F, Gas 4

Children will love these crisp
pizza triangles. Serve them
hot as an after-school snack,
warm at birthday parties and
cold in packed lunches. And,
of course, the toppings can
be changed to suit individual
tastes.

4 pitta bread rounds
1 cup/250 mL/8 fl oz prepared
tomato pasta sauce
1 green pepper, chopped
1 red onion, chopped
220 g/7 oz small prawns, peeled or
125 g/4 oz canned prawns, drained
3 tablespoons chopped pineapple pieces
125 g/4 oz salami, chopped
100 g/3 1/2 oz button mushrooms, sliced
125 g/4 oz grated mozzarella cheese

1 Spread each pitta bread round with
tomato pasta sauce, then top with green
pepper and onion.

2 Top two pitta bread rounds with
prawns and pineapple. Top the remaining
two with salami and mushrooms. Sprinkle
pizzas with cheese and bake for 20
minutes or until cheese is melted and
bread is crisp. Cut into triangles and
serve.

Serves 8

GRILLED GOAT'S CHEESE TOAST

1 radicchio, leaves separated
8 cherry tomatoes, halved
$^1/_2$ bunch/125 g/4 oz watercress, broken
into small sprigs
1 clove garlic, crushed
100 g/3$^1/_2$ oz goat's cheese
60 g/2 oz light cream cheese
freshly ground black pepper
8 slices bread, crusts trimmed

1   Arrange radicchio, tomatoes and
watercress on individual serving plates.

2   Place garlic, goat's cheese, cream
cheese and black pepper to taste in a bowl
and mix to combine. Set aside.

3   Toast bread slices, then spread with
cheese mixture. Place under a preheated
grill and cook for 2-3 minutes or until
cheese mixture is golden. Cut toast in half
diagonally and place 4 pieces on each
salad. Serve immediately.

Serves 4

These cheese toasts are
delicious made with rye or
grain bread.

MINI CARROT AND FETA QUICHES

Oven temperature
180°C, 350°F, Gas 4

500 g/1 lb prepared puff pastry

CARROT AND FETA FILLING
4 rashers bacon, finely chopped
4 spring onions, chopped
2 carrots, grated
125 g/4 oz feta cheese, crumbled
3 eggs
1 cup/250 mL/8 fl oz milk
125 g/4 oz grated tasty cheese
(mature Cheddar)
freshly ground black pepper

1 To make filling, cook bacon and spring onions in a frying pan over a medium heat for 4-5 minutes or until bacon is crisp. Add carrots and cook, stirring, for 2-3 minutes longer. Remove pan from heat and set aside to cool.

2 Place feta cheese, eggs, milk, tasty cheese (mature Cheddar) and black pepper to taste in a bowl and mix to combine. Stir in carrot mixture and set aside.

3 Roll out pastry and, using a 6 cm/ 2¹/₂ in biscuit cutter, cut out 24 rounds. Place rounds in lightly greased, shallow patty cake tins. Divide filling between pastry cases and bake for 15-20 minutes or until pastry is golden and filling is set.

Makes 24

Traditionally made from sheep's milk, feta cheese is crumbly and dripping with whey when fresh, but as it matures it becomes dry and somewhat salty.

BLUE CHEESE NIBBLES

1 cup/125 g/4 oz flour
$^1/_2$ teaspoon baking powder
pinch cayenne pepper
1 teaspoon dried mixed herbs
90 g/3 oz butter
90 g/3 oz blue cheese, crumbled
3 egg yolks
2 teaspoons water
celery salt or salt (optional)

1   Place flour, baking powder, cayenne pepper and mixed herbs in a food processor and process to sift. Add butter and blue cheese and process until mixture resembles coarse breadcrumbs. With machine running, slowly add egg yolks and water to form a dough. Turn dough onto a floured surface and knead until smooth.

2   Roll out dough to 5 mm/$^1/_4$ in thick and, using aspic cutters, cut out shapes or, using a sharp knife, cut into small squares, triangles or diamonds. Place shapes on lightly greased baking trays and bake for 8-10 minutes or until biscuits are lightly browned. Sprinkle with celery salt or salt, if desired. Allow biscuits to cool on trays.

Makes 100

Oven temperature
200°C, 400°F, Gas 6

These biscuits are delicious as a snack or served with cocktails or pre-dinner drinks.

41

FONDUES

One of the traditional dishes of Switzerland, the fondue was created to use up cheese that was left over after the long winter storage. A traditional fondue made with cheese and wine is one of life's great pleasures and all you need is a heavy-based sauce-pan or double boiler.

Swiss Cheese Fondue

Strawberry Roulé
Fondue

Classic Swiss Fondue

Highland Fondue

Curried Cheese
Fondue

Apple Cider Fondue

Swiss Cheese Fondue

Swiss Cheese Fondue

1 clove garlic, crushed
500 g/1 lb Gruyère cheese, grated
3 tablespoons potato flour
^{3}/4 cup/185 mL/6 fl oz dry white wine

1   Rub the inside of a fondue pot with crushed garlic. Place cheese, flour and wine in fondue pot and mix to combine.

2   Cook fondue over a medium heat, stirring constantly, until cheese melts and mixture is thick.

Serves 4

Did you know the word 'fondue' comes from the French word *fondre*, meaning 'to melt'?

Strawberry Roule Fondue

440 g/14 oz canned strawberries, drained
250 g/8 oz strawberry roulé cheese or cream cheese
^{2}/3 cup/155 mL/5 fl oz cream (double), whipped

Place strawberries and cheese in a food processor or blender and process to combine. Fold strawberry mixture into whipped cream and serve.

Serves 6

Really a dip rather than a fondue this dish is delicious served with fresh strawberries and cubes of almond or plain sponge.

'Gruyère cheese is made in both Switzerland and France and is the best cheese to use to make a Swiss Fondue. Gruyère is made in large wheels and is pale yellow in colour with a hard rind.'

FONDUE EQUIPMENT

Since the 1960s when fondue parties were popular there has been a variety of fondue sets consisting of a pot, stand, burner and forks. Many people may believe that one of these sets is essential for making a fondue. No so – in fact not even desirable in many cases.

In Switzerland, the home of the original cheese fondue, fondues are made in heavy cast-iron pots or earthenware pots known as caquelons. These pots are placed on a spirit or gas burner over a low, even heat so that the cheese melts into a smooth sauce.

When looking at fondue equipment beware of pots with thin metal bases as these have a tendency to cause the food to burn on the bottom. At home you can use a heavy-based pot placed over a portable gas cooker, a chafing dish or even a pot placed in an electric frying pan to make a fondue at the table. If you do not want to make the fondue at the table a cheese fondue can easily be made in a double boiler on the stove or cooker top. If you do not have long fondue forks, ordinary forks or bamboo skewers do the job just as well.

Traditionally a cheese fondue is prepared in front of your guests and it is a fun, informal way to entertain.

A selection of equipment suitable for fondue-making

CLASSIC SWISS FONDUE

1 clove garlic, halved
1 cup/250 mL/8 fl oz dry white wine
1 teaspoon lemon juice
250 g/8 oz grated Gruyère cheese
250 g/8 oz grated Emmenthal cheese
2 teaspoons cornflour
2 tablespoons Kirsch
freshly ground black pepper
ground nutmeg

1   Rub the inside of a fondue pot with garlic. Pour wine and lemon juice into fondue pot and cook over a medium heat until bubbling. Reduce heat to low and, using a wooden spoon, stir in Gruyère and Emmenthal cheeses. Continue stirring until cheeses melt.

2   Place cornflour and Kirsch in a small bowl and whisk to combine. Stir cornflour mixture into cheese mixture and cook, stirring constantly, for 2-3 minutes longer or until fondue is thick and smooth. Season to taste with black pepper and nutmeg. Serve immediately.

Serves 6

From top: Strawberry Roulé Fondue, Classic Swiss Fondue, Highland Fondue

You might like to do as the Swiss do and dip bread cubes into Kirsch before dipping them into the fondue – but be warned, this is not for the weak-hearted!

HIGHLAND FONDUE

15 g/½ oz butter
1 small onion, finely chopped
1 cup/250 mL/8 fl oz milk
500 g/1 lb grated tasty cheese
(mature Cheddar)
3 teaspoons cornflour
⅓ cup/90 mL/3 fl oz whisky

1 Melt butter in a large saucepan, add onion and cook over a medium heat for 5 minutes or until onion is soft. Stir in milk and bring to the boil.

2 Reduce heat, stir in cheese and cook, stirring constantly, until cheese is melted. Place cornflour and whisky in a small bowl and whisk to combine. Stir cornflour mixture into cheese mixture and cook, stirring constantly, for 2-3 minutes or until fondue is thick and smooth.

Serves 6

The secret to making a perfect fondue is to cook it over a low, even heat. The heat should be enough to melt the cheese and keep the fondue just bubbling but not so much that it causes the cheese to separate and become stringy.
This fondue is delicious served with cubes of rye bread.

CURRIED CHEESE FONDUE

1 clove garlic, halved
⅔ cup/170 mL/5½ fl oz dry white wine
1 teaspoon lemon juice
2 teaspoons curry paste
250 g/8 oz grated Gruyère cheese
185 g/6 oz grated tasty cheese
(mature Cheddar)
1 teaspoon cornflour
2 tablespoons dry sherry

1 Rub the inside of a fondue pot with garlic. Pour wine and lemon juice into fondue pot, place over a medium heat and cook until bubbling. Reduce heat to low, stir in curry paste, Gruyère cheese and tasty cheese (mature Cheddar) and cook, stirring constantly, until cheeses melt.

2 Place cornflour and sherry in a small bowl and whisk to combine. Stir cornflour mixture into cheese mixture and cook, stirring constantly, for 2-3 minutes or until fondue is thick and smooth.

Serves 6

A wine with a high acid content is good to use in making a fondue as the acid helps to melt the cheese. You might like to serve this fondue with Nan bread.

APPLE CIDER FONDUE

¹/₂ onion
1 cup/250 mL/8 fl oz dry cider
1 teaspoon lemon juice
375 g/12 oz grated tasty cheese
(mature Cheddar)
¹/₂ teaspoon dry mustard
3 teaspoons cornflour
¹/₄ cup/60 mL/2 fl oz apple juice
freshly ground black pepper

1   Rub the inside of a fondue pot with cut side of onion. Pour cider and lemon juice into fondue pot, place over a medium heat and cook until bubbling. Reduce heat to low, stir in cheese and cook, stirring constantly, until cheese is melted.

2   Place mustard, cornflour and apple juice in a small bowl and whisk to combine. Stir cornflour mixture into cheese mixture and cook, stirring constantly, for 2-3 minutes or until fondue is thick and smooth.

Serves 6

Serve this fondue with apple wedges and cubes of crusty bread.

Apple Cider Fondue

47

CHEESECAKES

A cheesecake is without doubt one of the best loved desserts. In this chapter you will find ten top cheesecakes – something to suit every taste and occasion.

Orange and Lime Cheesecake

Orange and Lime Cheesecake

155 g/5 oz plain sweet biscuits, crushed
90 g/3 oz butter, melted
desiccated coconut, toasted

ORANGE AND LIME FILLING
185 g/6 oz cream cheese, softened
2 tablespoons brown sugar
1^1/$_2$ teaspoons finely grated orange rind
1^1/$_2$ teaspoons finely grated lime rind
3 teaspoons orange juice
3 teaspoons lime juice
1 egg, lightly beaten
^{1}/$_2$ cup/125 mL/4 fl oz sweetened condensed milk
2 tablespoons cream (double), whipped

1 Place crushed biscuits and melted butter in a bowl and mix to combine. Press biscuit mixture over base and up sides of a well-greased 23 cm/9 in flan tin with a removable base. Bake for 5-8 minutes, then remove from oven and set aside to cool.

2 To make filling, place cream cheese, sugar, orange and lime rinds, and orange and lime juices in a bowl and beat until creamy. Beat in egg, then mix in condensed milk and fold in cream.

3 Spoon filling into prepared biscuit case and bake for 25-30 minutes or until filling is just firm. Turn oven off and allow cheesecake to cool in oven with door ajar. Chill before serving. Just prior to serving, sprinkle with coconut.

Serves 8

Oven temperature
180°C, 350°F, Gas 4

When limes are unavailable, lemon rind and lemon juice can be used instead of the lime rind and juice to make an equally delicious Orange and Lemon Cheesecake.

Chestnut Cheesecake

125 g/4 oz plain chocolate biscuits, crushed
60 g/2 oz butter, melted
125 g/4 oz white chocolate, grated
^{2}/$_3$ cup/155 mL/5 fl oz cream (double), whipped

CHESTNUT AND CHOCOLATE FILLING
375 g/12 oz ricotta cheese
1 cup/185 g/6 oz canned sweet chestnut purée
^{2}/$_3$ cup/170 mL/5^1/$_2$ fl oz cream (double)
125 g/4 oz white chocolate, broken into pieces
1^1/$_2$ tablespoons brandy
3 eggs
3 teaspoons flour

1 Place crushed biscuits and melted butter in a bowl and mix to combine. Press biscuit mixture over base of a well-greased 20 cm/8 in springform tin.

2 To make filling, place ricotta cheese and chestnut purée in a bowl and beat to combine. Place cream in a small saucepan and bring to the boil over a medium heat. Remove pan from heat, add chocolate pieces and stir until chocolate is melted. Stir in brandy, then stir cream mixture into cheese mixture. Add eggs and flour and beat well to combine.

3 Spoon filling into prepared cake tin and bake for 1 hour. Allow cheesecake to cool in tin. Just prior to serving, sprinkle cheesecake with grated chocolate and pipe a border of whipped cream rosettes around the edge.

Serves 10

Oven temperature
180°C, 350°F, Gas 4

For an extra-special decoration you might like to decorate the top of this cheesecake with candied chestnut pieces rolled in caster sugar and crystallised angelica leaves.

CHOC-WHISKY CHEESECAKE

Oven temperature
180°C, 350°F, Gas 4

When preparing a springform
tin for a cheesecake, turn the
base upside down and
cover it with foil. This will
make the base much easier
to remove.

185 g/6 oz ginger biscuits, crushed
60 g/2 oz butter, melted
2 tablespoons cocoa powder
1 tablespoon icing sugar
1/2 teaspoon ground ginger

CHOC-WHISKY FILLING
750 g/1 1/2 lb cream cheese
1/4 cup/45 g/1 1/2 oz brown sugar
2 eggs
1 1/2 tablespoons cocoa powder, sifted
2 teaspoons ground ginger
2/3 cup/170 mL/5 1/2 fl oz cream (double)
250 g/8 oz dark chocolate, broken
into pieces
1/3 cup/90 mL/3 fl oz whisky

1   Place crushed biscuits and melted
butter in a bowl and mix to combine.
Press biscuit mixture over base of a well-
greased 20 cm/8 in springform tin.

2   To make filling, place cream cheese,
brown sugar and eggs in a bowl and beat
well to combine. Beat in cocoa powder
and ground ginger.

3   Place cream in a small saucepan and
bring to the boil. Remove pan from heat,
add chocolate and stir until chocolate is
melted. Stir in whisky, then stir cream
mixture into cheese mixture.

4   Spoon filling into prepared cake tin
and bake for 45 minutes. Allow
cheesecake to cool in tin. Just prior to
serving, decorate cheesecake.

5   To decorate, cut five strips of
greaseproof paper each 2 cm/3/4 in wide
and lay them, evenly spaced, over surface
of cheesecake. Place cocoa powder, icing
sugar and ground ginger in a small bowl
and mix to combine, then sift over top of
cheesecake. Carefully remove strips of
paper before serving.

Serves 8

BOSTON CHEESECAKE

250 g/8 oz plain sweet biscuits, crushed
¹/4 teaspoon ground cinnamon
¹/4 teaspoon ground allspice
60 g/2 oz butter, melted
icing sugar

SOUR CREAM FILLING
500 g/1 lb cream cheese
1 cup/250 g/8 oz sour cream
²/3 cup/140 g/4¹/2 oz caster sugar
4 eggs, separated
2 tablespoons flour
¹/4 teaspoon vanilla essence
2 teaspoons finely grated lemon rind
2 tablespoons lemon juice

1   Place crushed biscuits, cinnamon, allspice and melted butter in a bowl and mix to combine. Press biscuit mixture over base of a well-greased 23 cm/9 in springform tin.

2   To make filling, place cream cheese, sour cream, one-third caster sugar, egg yolks, flour, vanilla essence, lemon rind and lemon juice in a large bowl and beat to combine.

3   Place egg whites in a large bowl and beat until soft peaks form. Gradually add remaining caster sugar, beating well after each addition until stiff peaks form. Fold egg white mixture into cheese mixture, spoon into prepared cake tin and bake for 1 hour. Allow cheesecake to cool in tin. Just prior to serving, decorate cheesecake.

4   To decorate, cut five strips of greaseproof paper each 2 cm/³/4 in wide and lay them, evenly spaced, over surface of cheesecake. Sift icing sugar over top of cheesecake. Carefully remove strips of paper before serving.

Serves 10

Oven temperature
180°C, 350°F, Gas 4

Cream cheese and cottage cheese are two of the oldest known forms of cheese. They were made in the days before the ripening process was discovered.

From left: Chestnut Cheesecake, Choc-Whisky Cheesecake, Boston Cheesecake

CHEESECAKE FINGERS

Oven temperature
160°C, 325°F, Gas 3

The manufacturing processes
for making cream cheese
and cottage cheese are
somewhat similar. However,
cream cheese is made from
cream or a mixture of cream
and milk, while cottage
cheese is made from skim
milk.

BASE
1 cup/125 g/4 oz flour
³/4 cup/90 g/3 oz self-raising flour
¹/4 cup/60 g/2 oz caster sugar
125 g/4 oz chilled butter, cut into pieces
2 egg yolks, beaten

FRUIT FILLING
500 g/1 lb cream cheese
²/3 cup/170 g/5¹/2 fl oz sour cream
2 eggs
¹/2 cup/100 g/3¹/2 oz caster sugar
2 tablespoons semolina
30 g/1 oz sultanas
30 g/1 oz raisins
30 g/1 oz glacé cherries, chopped
30 g/1 oz mixed peel
1 tablespoon flour
2 teaspoons finely grated orange rind
2 tablespoons orange juice

APRICOT GLAZE
2 tablespoons apricot jam
1 tablespoon water

1   To make base, place flour, self-raising
flour and sugar in a food processor and
process to sift. Add butter and process
until mixture resembles coarse
breadcrumbs. With machine running, add
egg yolks and process until a soft dough
forms. Turn dough onto a floured surface
and knead briefly. Wrap dough in plastic
food wrap and refrigerate for 15 minutes.
Roll dough out to 5 mm/¹/4 in thick and
line the base and sides of a well-greased
square 23 cm/9 in cake tin. Refrigerate
while making filling.

2   To make filling, place cream cheese,
sour cream, eggs, sugar and semolina in a
bowl and beat until smooth. Place
sultanas, raisins, cherries, mixed peel and
flour in a separate bowl and toss to coat
fruit with flour. Stir fruit mixture, orange
rind and orange juice into cheese mixture.
Spoon filling into prepared cake tin and
bake for 1 hour or until the cake is cooked
when tested with a skewer.

3   For the glaze, place apricot jam and
water in a small saucepan and bring to the
boil, brush over hot cheesecake and set
aside to cool.

Serves 12

This page: Cheesecake Fingers
Opposite page: Strawberry Slice

STRAWBERRY SLICE

Oven temperature
200°C, 400°F, Gas 6

1/2 cup/60 g/2 oz flour
1/2 cup/75 g/2 1/2 oz wholemeal flour
60 g/2 oz butter
1 egg yolk
2 tablespoons apple juice

CHEESECAKE FILLING
250 g/8 oz ricotta cheese
1/2 cup/100 g/3 1/2 oz natural yogurt
2 eggs
2 tablespoons lemon juice
1/4 cup/60 g/2 oz sugar

STRAWBERRY TOPPING
250 g/8 oz strawberries
3/4 cup/185 mL/6 fl oz cream (double),
whipped

1   Place flour, wholemeal flour and butter in a food processor and process until mixture resembles fine breadcrumbs. With machine running, add egg yolk and enough apple juice to form a soft dough. Turn dough onto a floured surface and knead lightly. Press dough over base of a well-greased 23 cm/9 in springform tin. Line pastry case with nonstick baking paper, fill with uncooked rice and bake for 8-10 minutes. Remove paper and rice and bake for 8-10 minutes longer or until pastry is golden. Set aside to cool.

2   To make filling, place ricotta cheese, yogurt, eggs, lemon juice and sugar in a bowl and beat until smooth. Spoon filling over pastry base and bake at 180°C/ 350°F/Gas 4 for 30 minutes or until filling is firm. Remove slice from oven and set aside to cool.

3   For the topping, place half the strawberries in a food processor or blender and process to make a purée. Push purée through a sieve to remove seeds, then spread over top of cold slice. Just prior to serving, decorate top of cheesecake with whipped cream and remaining strawberries.

Serves 10

Ricotta is made from the whey left over after making semi-hard cheese. This whey contains a protein called lactalbumin and when heated it coagulates and can be separated from the whey. This is the basic principal used in the making of ricotta cheese.

BASIC CHEESECAKE

Oven temperature
120°C, 250°F, Gas $^1/_2$

BASE
**200 g/6$^1/_2$ oz plain sweet biscuits,
crushed
125 g/4 oz butter, melted
1 teaspoon mixed spice
$^1/_2$ teaspoon ground ginger**

FILLING
**250 g/8 oz cream cheese
250 g/8 oz ricotta cheese
$^2/_3$ cup/170 g/5$^1/_2$ oz caster sugar
3 eggs
$^1/_4$ cup/30 g/1 oz flour, sifted
1 tablespoon lemon juice
1 teaspoon vanilla essence
$^3/_4$ cup/185 mL/6 fl oz cream (double)**

1 To make base, place crushed biscuits, butter, mixed spice and ginger in a bowl and mix well to combine. Press over the base and up sides of a greased 20 cm/8 in springform tin. Refrigerate until firm.

2 To make filling, place cream cheese, ricotta cheese and sugar in a bowl and beat until sugar dissolves. Add eggs one at a time, beating well after each addition. Fold in flour, then lemon juice, vanilla essence and cream.

3 Spoon filling into prepared tin and bake for 1$^1/_2$ hours or until the cheesecake is just firm in the centre. Turn off the oven, leave cheesecake to cool in oven with door ajar. Refrigerate for several hours or overnight before serving.

Serves 8

VARIATIONS

*For all these variations the basic method and ingredients stay
the same. All cheesecakes serve 8.*

**Double Chocolate and Pecan
Cheesecake:** Make the base using plain sweet chocolate biscuits, omitting the mixed spice and ginger. For the filling, omit the lemon juice and fold 155 g/5 oz melted dark chocolate and 100 g/3$^1/_2$ oz chopped pecans in with the cream. Complete as directed in the basic recipe.

Ginger Honey Cheesecake: Omit the mixed spice from the base and add 1 extra teaspoon ground ginger. For the filling, replace 3 tablespoons caster sugar with 3 tablespoons honey. Toss 100 g/3$^1/_2$ oz finely chopped glacé ginger in a little flour and fold into the filling with the cream. Complete as directed in the basic recipe.

**Strawberry and Passion Fruit
Cheesecake:** Arrange 250 g/8 oz hulled and quartered strawberries over the biscuit base and fold the pulp of 4 passion fruit or $^1/_4$ cup/60 mL/2 fl oz passion fruit pulp into the filling with the cream. Complete as directed in the basic recipe.

Basic Cheesecake, Double Chocolate and
Pecan Cheesecake

DESSERTS

Cheeses such as ricotta, cottage and cream are ideal for making desserts. In this chapter you will find a variety of desserts that make the most of these cheeses. For something savoury to finish a meal you might like to serve the Stilton Grapes.

Strawberry Hearts

Strawberry Hearts

250 g/8 oz strawberries, quartered
$^1/_4$ cup/45 g/1$^1/_2$ oz icing sugar
250 g/8 oz ricotta cheese
$^1/_2$ cup/125 mL/4 fl oz cream (double)
2 teaspoons gelatine dissolved in
$^1/_4$ cup/60 mL/2 fl oz hot orange juice,
cooled to room temperature

1 Place strawberries, icing sugar, ricotta cheese and cream in a food processor or blender and process until smooth.

2 Stir gelatine mixture into strawberry mixture and mix to combine.

3 Rinse four heart-shaped moulds in cold water and line with muslin or gauze. Spoon strawberry mixture into moulds, cover and refrigerate until set. To serve, turn hearts onto serving plates.

Serves 4

The gelatine mixture and the strawberry mixture should be the same temperature. This will prevent the desserts from separating into two layers.

Rhubarb and Apple Tart

PASTRY
1 cup/125 g/4 oz flour
2 teaspoons icing sugar
90 g/3 oz butter, cubed
3-4 teaspoons iced water

RHUBARB AND APPLE FILLING
6 stalks rhubarb, chopped
2 tablespoons sugar
30 g/1 oz butter
3 green apples, cored, peeled and sliced
125 g/4 oz cream cheese
$^1/_3$ cup/75 g/2$^1/_2$ oz caster sugar
1 teaspoon vanilla essence
1 egg

1 To make pastry, place flour and icing sugar in a food processor and process to sift. Add butter and process until mixture resembles coarse breadcrumbs. With machine running, add water and continue to process until a smooth dough forms. Turn dough onto a lightly floured surface and knead briefly. Wrap in plastic food wrap and refrigerate for 30 minutes.

2 Roll out dough on a lightly floured surface and use to line a greased 23 cm/ 9 in fluted flan tin with a removable base. Line pastry case with nonstick baking paper, fill with uncooked rice and bake for 15 minutes. Remove rice and paper and bake for 5 minutes longer or until pastry is golden. Set aside to cool.

3 To make filling, poach or microwave rhubarb until tender. Drain well, stir in sugar and set aside to cool. Melt butter in a frying pan and cook apples for 3-4 minutes. Remove apples from pan and set aside to cool.

4 Place cream cheese, caster sugar, vanilla essence and egg in a bowl and beat until smooth. Spoon rhubarb into pastry case, then top with cream cheese mixture and arrange apple slices attractively on the top. Reduce oven temperature to 180°C/350°F/Gas 4 and cook for 40-45 minutes or until filling is firm.

Serves 8

Oven temperature
200°C, 400°F, Gas 6

A light cream cheese is available which is a mixture of cream and cottage cheese. This is a good alternative for those watching fat and kilojoule (calorie) intake as it can be successfully used in place of standard cream cheese.

ROQUEFORT TART

Oven temperature
200°C, 400°F, Gas 6

Roquefort is a blue cheese
made from sheep's milk. It
comes from the village of
Roquefort-sur-Soulzon in the
south of France. The cheese
gets its unique characteristics
from being matured in the
limestone caves that are
situated near the village.
Only cheese matured in the
limestone caves near
Roquefort-sur-Soulzon can be
called Roquefort. If Roquefort
cheese is unavailable you
could use another blue
cheese in its place for this
recipe.

CREAM CHEESE PASTRY
250 g/8 oz cream cheese
250 g/8 oz butter
1 cup/125 g/4 oz flour
1/4 cup/60 g/2 oz caster sugar
1 teaspoon ground mixed spice

ROQUEFORT FILLING
1 cup/250 mL/8 fl oz cream (double)
125 g/4 oz Roquefort cheese, crumbled
4 tablespoons chopped pecans or
walnuts
2 eggs, beaten

1   To make pastry, roughly chop cream
cheese and butter and set aside to stand at
room temperature for 10 minutes. Place
flour, sugar and mixed spice in a food
processor and process briefly to sift. Add
cream cheese and butter and process,
using the pulse button, until mixture is
combined. Take care not to overmix the
dough. Turn dough onto a lightly floured
surface, gather into a ball and knead

briefly. Wrap in plastic food wrap and
refrigerate for at least 1 hour.

2   Roll out dough on a lightly floured
surface to 5 mm/1/4 in thick and line base
and sides of well-greased 23 cm/9 in flan
tin with removable base. Line pastry case
with nonstick baking paper, fill with
uncooked rice and bake for 10 minutes.
Remove rice and paper and bake for 5
minutes longer or until pastry is golden.
Set aside to cool.

3   To make filling, place cream and
Roquefort cheese in a saucepan and cook
over a medium heat, stirring constantly,
until cheese melts. Remove pan from
heat and set aside to cool. Stir in pecans
and eggs, then pour filling into pastry case
and bake for 20 minutes or until filling is
set.

Serves 6

CHOCOLATE LOG

185 g/6 oz butter
1/4 cup/30 g/1 oz cocoa powder
1 cup/250 mL/8 fl oz hot water
200 g/6 1/2 oz dark chocolate, chopped
1 cup/220 g/7 oz caster sugar
125 g/4 oz ricotta cheese
3/4 cup/90 g/3 oz flour
1 cup/125 g/4 oz self-raising flour
2 eggs

CHOCOLATE FILLING
200 g/6 1/2 oz milk chocolate, melted
2 tablespoons cream (double)
60 g/2 oz chopped nuts

CHOCOLATE ICING
125 g/4 oz dark chocolate
30 g/1 oz butter

1   Place butter, cocoa powder, water, chocolate and sugar in a saucepan and cook over a medium heat, stirring constantly, until chocolate melts and ingredients are combined.

2   Transfer chocolate mixture to a large bowl. Beat in ricotta cheese, flour, self-raising flour and eggs. Continue beating until mixture is smooth. Spoon mixture into a greased and lined 11 x 21 cm/ 4 1/2 x 8 1/2 in loaf tin and bake for 1 1/2 hours or until cake is cooked when tested with a skewer. Allow cake to stand in tin for 5 minutes before turning onto a wire rack to cool completely.

3   To make filling, place chocolate, cream and nuts in a bowl and mix to combine. Cut cake horizontally into three layers. Spread two of the layers with filling, place one on top of the other, then top with the plain layer.

4   To make icing, place chocolate and butter in a heatproof bowl over a saucepan of simmering water and heat, stirring, until chocolate melts and mixture is smooth. Spread top and sides of cake with icing and refrigerate until set.

Serves 10

Oven temperature
160°C, 325°F, Gas 3

For a special occasion this dessert is delicious served with whipped cream and fresh raspberries.

'In Italy Ricotta can be made from cow's or sheep's milk. If made from sheep's milk it is known ricotta pecora if from cow's milk ricotta vaccina.'

Roquefort Tart

Dark Chocolate Cake

Oven temperature
160°C, 325°F, Gas 3

$^3/_4$ cup/75 g/2$^1/_2$ oz cocoa powder
$^3/_4$ cup/185 mL/6 fl oz boiling water
1$^3/_4$ cups/220 g/7 oz self-raising flour
1$^1/_2$ cups/330 g/10$^1/_2$ oz caster sugar
6 eggs, separated
60 g/2 oz butter, melted

CREAM CHEESE FILLING
1$^1/_4$ cups/200 g/6$^1/_2$ oz icing sugar
$^1/_4$ cup/60 mL/2 fl oz milk
1 teaspoon vanilla essence
2 tablespoons cocoa powder
250 g/8 oz cream cheese, softened

DECORATION
125 g/4 oz chopped nuts
125 g/4 oz milk chocolate
1 tablespoon butter
1 cup/250 mL/8 fl oz cream (double),
whipped
90 g/3 oz whole hazelnuts

This rich chocolate cake
makes the ideal adult
birthday cake.

1 Place cocoa powder in a small bowl. Gradually add boiling water to make a smooth paste. Place flour and sugar in a large bowl, add cocoa mixture, egg yolks and butter and beat until smooth.

2 Place egg whites in a large bowl and beat until soft peaks form. Fold egg white mixture into cocoa. Spoon batter into a greased and lined 23 cm/9 in springform tin and bake for 1 hour or until cake is cooked when tested with a skewer. Allow cake to cool in tin for 5 minutes then turn onto a wire rack to cool completely.

3 To make filling, place icing sugar, milk, vanilla essence and cocoa in a bowl and mix to make a smooth paste. Place cream cheese and cocoa mixture in a food processor or blender and process until smooth. Remove 6 tablespoons of filling and set aside – this is used for the sides of the cake.

4 Cut cake horizontally into three layers. spread two of the layers with filling, place one on top of the other, then top with the plain layer. Spread reserved filling around sides of cake. Chill cake for 1 hour or until filling is set.

5 To decorate the cake, place chopped nuts on a piece of greaseproof paper and roll cake in nuts to coat sides. Place milk chocolate and butter in a heatproof bowl over a saucepan of simmering water and heat, stirring, until chocolate melts and mixture is smooth. Spread top of cake with chocolate mixture and refrigerate until set. Just prior to serving, pipe rosettes of whipped cream around edge of cake and place a whole hazelnut in the middle of each rosette.

Serves 10

Dark Chocolate Cake,
Chocolate Log

ORANGE FIGS

8 glacé figs

ORANGE CHEESE FILLING
155 g/5 oz cream cheese, softened
2 teaspoons finely grated orange rind
2 tablespoons orange-flavoured liqueur
$^1/_4$ cup/45 g/1$^1/_2$ oz icing sugar

ORANGE SYRUP
$^1/_2$ cup/125 mL/4 fl oz orange juice
1 tablespoon lemon juice
2 tablespoons caster sugar

Glacé figs are available from health food shops. This filling is also delicious with other glacé fruits such as apricots and peaches.

1 To make filling, place cream cheese, orange rind, liqueur and icing sugar in a bowl and beat to combine. Make a slit in each fig and spoon in 2 tablespoons of filling. Chill for at least 1 hour.

2 To make syrup, place orange juice, lemon juice and sugar in a small saucepan, bring to the boil over a low heat and simmer for 5 minutes. Remove pan from heat and set aside to cool for 15 minutes. Serve syrup spooned over figs.

Serves 4

CHOCOLATE TIRAMISU

2 eggs, separated
$^1/_2$ cup/100 g/3$^1/_2$ oz caster sugar
1$^1/_2$ cups/375 g/12 oz mascarpone
$^1/_4$ cup/60 mL/2 fl oz brandy
200 g/6$^1/_2$ oz sponge finger biscuits
$^1/_4$ cup/60 mL/2 fl oz very strong black coffee
$^1/_4$ cup/30 g/1 oz cocoa powder, sifted

1   Place egg yolks and sugar in a bowl and beat until light and fluffy. Add mascarpone and brandy and beat until mixture is smooth.

2   Place egg whites in a clean bowl and beat until soft peaks form. Carefully fold egg white mixture into egg yolk mixture.

3   Place half the sponge finger biscuits in the base of a large serving bowl, sprinkle with half the coffee and top with half the mascarpone mixture. Repeat layers and dust top of dessert with cocoa powder.

Serves 8

Mascarpone is a fresh cheese made from cream. It is unsalted, buttery and rich with a fat content of 90 per cent and mostly is used as a dessert, either alone or as an ingredient.
Mascarpone is available from delicatessens and some supermarkets. If it is unavailable, mix one part sour cream to three parts lightly whipped cream (double) and use in its place.

BRIE AND BRIOCHE

375 g/12 oz raspberries
200 g/6¹/₂ oz wedge Brie cheese, cut
into 4 equal pieces
1 round plain brioche, thinly sliced and
toasted
8 dried figs, sliced

Brie achieved worldwide
fame when it was crowned
'King of Cheeses' at the
Vienna Congress of 1814 and
1815. It was originally a
farmhouse cheese that took
the name Brie from the
region of the same name
in France.

1   Place 250 g/8 oz raspberries in a food
processor or blender and process until
smooth. Push purée through a fine sieve
to remove seeds.

2   Place a piece of Brie and a little
raspberry purée on four serving plates.
Arrange brioche, figs and remaining
raspberries attractively on plates. Serve
immediately.

Serves 4

STILTON GRAPES

125 g/4 oz cream cheese, softened
60 g/2 oz Stilton cheese, crumbled
2 tablespoons sour cream
30 large seedless green grapes
125 g/4 oz chopped pistachio nuts

1   Place cream cheese, Stilton and sour cream in a bowl and beat until smooth.

2   Wrap each grape in a little cream cheese mixture then roll in pistachio nuts to coat. Refrigerate until firm.

Makes 30

'To serve these delicious morsels you might like to arrange them in the shape of a bunch of grapes. If you have either a real or ornamental grape vine, use some of the leaves to decorate the plate.'

*This page: Stilton Grapes
Left: Brie and Brioche*

CHEESY MUSHROOM SLICE

Oven temperature
180°C, 350°F, Gas 4

60 g/2 oz butter
3 rashers bacon, chopped
440 g/14 oz mushrooms, sliced
4 spring onions, chopped
1 small green pepper, chopped
1 small red pepper, chopped
6 thick slices white bread,
crusts removed
125 g/4 oz grated tasty cheese
(mature Cheddar)
6 eggs
2 cups/500 mL/16 fl oz milk
1 tablespoon mayonnaise
1 teaspoon French mustard
1 teaspoon Worcestershire sauce
2 tablespoons chopped fresh parsley

1   Melt butter in a large frying pan, add bacon and cook for 4-5 minutes or until crisp. Stir in mushrooms, spring onions and green and red peppers and cook for 5 minutes longer or until mushrooms are soft.

2   Cut bread slices into 2.5 cm/1 in pieces. Place half the bread in the base of a lightly greased 18 x 28 cm/7 x 11 in ovenproof dish. Spoon mushroom mixture over and top with remaining bread. Sprinkle with cheese.

3   Place eggs, milk, mayonnaise, mustard and Worcestershire sauce in a bowl and whisk to combine. Carefully pour egg mixture over bread mixture and sprinkle with parsley. Bake for 50-60 minutes or until slice is firm.

This recipe is an ideal one to cook ahead. Prepare the whole dish, and refrigerate overnight. Bake when you are ready the next day. The flavour develops if you allow the slice to stand before cooking.

Serves 6

Cheesy Mushroom Slice

CHEESE STRAWS AND PLAITS

Oven temperature
200°C, 400°F, Gas 6

1 cup/125 g/4 oz flour
$^1/_2$ teaspoon baking powder
$^1/_4$ teaspoon salt
$^1/_4$ teaspoon cayenne pepper or to taste
$^1/_4$ teaspoon dry mustard
90 g/3 oz grated Parmesan cheese
90 g/3 oz butter
3 egg yolks
2 teaspoons cold water
1 egg white, lightly beaten
paprika

The straws look attractive served in a pastry ring. To make a pastry ring, cut a circle using a 6 cm/2$^1/_2$ in biscuit cutter, then cut out the centre to form a ring using a 4.5 cm/1$^3/_4$ in biscuit cutter. Bake as for straws and plaits.

1   Place flour, baking powder, salt, cayenne pepper and mustard in a food processor and process to sift. Reserve 3 teaspoons Parmesan cheese and set aside. Add butter and remaining Parmesan cheese to flour mixture and process until mixture resembles fine breadcrumbs. With machine running, slowly add egg yolks and water to form a dough.

2   Turn dough onto a lightly floured surface and knead briefly. Roll out dough to a rectangle 23 x 30 cm/9 x 12 in. Trim edges and brush dough with egg white, then sprinkle with reserved Parmesan cheese. Cut dough in half lengthwise, then into 5 mm/$^1/_4$ in strips crosswise. To make plaits, plait two strips together.

3   Place straws or plaits on lightly greased baking trays and bake for 8-10 minutes or until straws or plaits are lightly browned. Allow to cool on trays for 2-3 minutes before transferring to a wire rack to cool completely. When cold, dust straws or plaits with paprika.

Makes 100 straws or 50 plaits

CRUNCHY CAMEMBERT

3 x 125 g/4 oz wheels Camembert
cheese
2 teaspoons flour
$^1/_2$ teaspoon dry mustard
$^1/_2$ teaspoon dried mixed herbs
freshly ground black pepper
$^1/_4$ cup/30 g/1 oz dried breadcrumbs
$^1/_2$ teaspoon chilli powder or to taste
1 egg, beaten
vegetable oil for deep-frying

BLUEBERRY SAUCE
2 teaspoons cornflour
$^1/_3$ cup/90 mL/3 fl oz water
250 g/8 oz fresh or frozen blueberries
$^1/_4$ cup/60 g/2 oz sugar
$^1/_4$ teaspoon ground nutmeg
2 teaspoons lemon juice

1   Cut each Camembert wheel into four equal portions, wrap each portion in plastic food wrap and freeze for 1 hour.

2   Place flour, mustard, mixed herbs and black pepper to taste in a small bowl and mix to combine. Place breadcrumbs and chilli powder on a plate and mix to combine. Roll each Camembert portion in flour mixture to coat, then dip in egg and roll in breadcrumb mixture. Place on a plate lined with plastic food wrap and freeze for 15 minutes longer.

3   Heat oil in a large saucepan until a cube of bread dropped in browns in 50 seconds. Cook cheese portions a few at time for 30 seconds or until golden. Remove, using a slotted spoon, and drain on absorbent kitchen paper.

4   To make sauce, place cornflour and water in a small saucepan and mix to combine. Stir in blueberries, sugar, nutmeg and lemon juice and cook over a medium heat, stirring constantly, for 4-5 minutes or until sauce thickens. Serve sauce warm with fried Camembert.

Serves 6

The secret to frying Camembert is to have it really cold before you start so that the outside cooks and forms a golden crust that hides a barely melting centre.

STUFFED CHEESE TOMATOES

24 cherry tomatoes

BLUE CHEESE FILLING
90 g/3 oz soft blue cheese
60 g/2 oz cottage cheese
2 tablespoons snipped fresh chives
freshly ground black pepper

ALMOND HERB FILLING
125 g/4 oz cream cheese
4 tablespoons slivered almonds, toasted
1 tablespoon chopped fresh mint
1 tablespoon chopped fresh parsley
1 tablespoon snipped fresh chives

1   Using a sharp knife, cut tops from tomatoes. Reserve tops. Scoop out seeds, using a small spoon, and turn tomatoes upside down on absorbent kitchen paper to drain.

2   To make Blue Cheese Filling, place blue cheese, cottage cheese, chives and black pepper to taste in a food processor or blender and process until smooth.

3   To make Almond Herb Filling, place cream cheese in a bowl and beat until smooth. Stir in almonds, mint, parsley, chives and black pepper to taste.

4   Using a small spoon, pack half the tomatoes with Blue Cheese Filling and half with Almond Herb Filling. Cover with reserved tops and chill until ready to serve.

Makes 24

Stuffed cherry tomatoes are popular as a pre-dinner snack or look attractive as part of a cold meat and salad platter.

Stuffed Cherry Tomatoes

CHEESE SAUCE

90 g/3 oz tasty cheese (mature Cheddar)
30 g/1 oz butter
2 tablespoons flour
1 cup/250 mL/8 fl oz milk
$^1/_2$ teaspoon dry mustard
3-4 drops Tabasco sauce
$^1/_4$ cup/60 mL/2 fl oz dry sherry
freshly ground black pepper

The secret to making a good cheese sauce is to add the cheese right at the end of the cooking time. After the cheese is added, very little additional cooking is required as the heat of the sauce melts the cheese almost immediately. If the sauce is heated for too long after the cheese is added the cheese will become tough and stringy.
If making the sauce in advance, add the cheese after reheating the sauce.

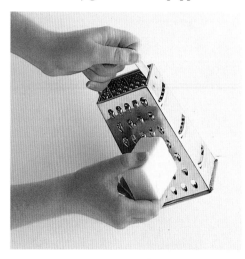

1   Grate cheese and set aside. Melt butter in a heavy-based saucepan, stir in flour and cook over a medium heat, stirring constantly, for 1 minute or until mixture is bubbly.

2   Using a wire whisk gradually whisk milk into flour mixture and cook, stirring constantly, to make a creamy sauce. Stir in mustard, Tabasco sauce, sherry and black pepper to taste and cook, stirring constantly, until sauce boils and thickens.

3   Add cheese to sauce and stir until cheese melts. Remove sauce from heat and serve immediately.

Makes 1$^1/_2$ cups/375 mL/12 fl oz

FETA CHEESE PASTRIES

3 eggs, lightly beaten
3 tablespoons chopped fresh parsley
freshly ground black pepper
500 g/1 lb feta cheese, crumbled
8 sheets filo pastry
125 g/4 oz butter, melted

3 Bring pastry up around the filling and squeeze to resemble a bag. Brush with butter and place on a lightly greased baking tray. Repeat with remaining pastry and cheese mixture. Bake pastries for 20-25 minutes or until golden. Serve immediately.

Oven temperature
200°C, 400°F, Gas 6

1 Place eggs, parsley and black pepper to taste in a bowl and whisk to combine. Stir in cheese and mix well.

Makes 16

When using filo pastry keep the pastry not being used covered with damp absorbent kitchen paper or a clean damp cloth. This prevents the pastry from drying out and cracking.

For a better shape, you might like to cook these pastries in lightly greased muffin tins or deep patty tins.

2 Take 1 sheet of pastry and cut in half. Brush each half with melted butter and fold each piece in half. Place a spoonful of cheese mixture in the centre of each piece.

TYPES OF CHEESES

There are so many different cheeses that it would be impossible to describe them all. This section looks at some of the more popular cheeses and the best way to store and keep them.

In Tuscany a dish known as '*ricotta umbriaca*' (drunken ricotta) is popular. This is ricotta laced with brandy or rum.

BLUE CHEESES

The three great blue cheeses are Roquefort from France, Stilton from England and the Italian cheese Gorgonzola, however nearly every country has its own blue cheese. Although they vary in taste and texture they all have a network of bluish veins of mould, due to the growth of Penicillium moulds within the cheese, and they tend to have a strong characteristic taste and smell.

BRIE

This is a creamy ripened soft cheese with a surface mould. Brie is mentioned in the Court of Champagne records, dated 1217. Ideal for serving as part of a cheese platter, Brie is also delicious served with fresh berries, fruit breads, nuts or grapes. To serve a whole Brie, cut it into wedges then cut each wedge into chunks.

CAMEMBERT

Similar to Brie, Camembert is traditionally a smaller round of cheese with a lower moisture content. Deep-fried Camembert is a popular restaurant dish. Camembert is a popular dessert cheese which teams well with fruit and fruit sauces. To serve a whole Camembert, cut it into thin wedges.

CHEDDAR CHEESES

These range in flavour from mild to sharp and, depending on the country, carry a variety of names. Tasty or mature Cheddar is one of the most popular everyday cheeses for eating and cooking and there would be few households that did not have a block of this in the refrigerator. Serve Cheddar at room temperature cut into slices or small cubes.

COTTAGE CHEESE

Legend tells of the discovery of cottage cheese. According to the story, a herdsman was carrying milk in a bag made from the stomach of a recently killed animal. As he travelled across the desert, the heat of the sun, the rennin from the stomach and the constant movement caused the milk to separate. So when the herdsman stopped to drink his milk he found that he had curds and whey. The curd, of course, was what we would call cottage cheese.

Cottage cheese with just 3 per cent fat is the favoured cheese of dieters the world over, however it is also a great cooking cheese and is the major ingredient in many cheesecakes and other cheese desserts.

CREAM CHEESE

One of the oldest forms of cheese, cream cheese is fresh unripened curd cheese made from cream. It is a smooth rich cheese with a mild flavour and good body. There are many different types, ranging from light cream cheese through to double and triple cream cheeses. The standard cream cheese is high in both kilojoules (calories) and fat. For those wishing to reduce fat and kilojoules (calories) in a recipe, cottage cheese or ricotta can often be substituted.

EDAM

This round ball-shaped cheese coated in red wax is an uncooked semi-hard cheese with a mild buttery flavour and a firm texture. Originating from Holland it dates back to the Middle Ages and takes its name from the town of Edam in northern Holland. Lower in fat than

Cheddar cheese, this cheese has excellent keeping qualities but does not melt as readily in cooking. Often classified by size, Edam ranges from 880 g/28 oz (Baby Edam) to 6.5 kg/13 lb (middlebare).

FETA

Most frequently used in cooking, feta cheese is white in colour with a salty taste. Matured in brine, feta is an uncooked soft cheese that was originally made from sheep's or goat's milk. Today however feta is often made from cow's milk. Another of the ancient cheeses, it has been made in the Balkans for centuries and it appears in many Greek myths.

GOUDA

Believed to have originated in the thirteenth century, this semi-hard uncooked curd cheese is one of the oldest Dutch cheeses and takes its name from the town of the same name. Produced as wheels and coated in yellow wax, Gouda was traditionally made by the women on the farms. Similar in appearance to Edam, it has a slightly higher fat content, is more creamy in texture and has a deeper flavour. Gouda is the cheese used for the Dutch fondue-style dish *kaasdoop*.

MASCARPONE

This fresh cheese made from cream is unsalted and buttery with a fat content of 90 per cent. It is mostly used as a dessert cheese, either alone or as an ingredient. If it is unavailable, mix one part thick sour cream with three parts lightly whipped cream (double), or beat 250 g/8 oz ricotta cheese with 250 mL/8 fl oz cream (single) until the mixture is smooth and thick.

MOZZARELLA

Mozzarella was once made almost exclusively from buffalo milk; today cow's milk is more commonly used. Real mozzarella is enjoyed as a table cheese when fresh and moist. As it ages and dries, it is only good for cooking, but its excellent melting qualities are retained. Mozzarella is the traditional pizza cheese and is available in a variety of shapes and sizes.

PARMESAN

Taking its name from the town of Parma in northern Italy, Parmesan cheese is a hard granular cheese with a grainy texture. It is a hard-cooked curd cheese and is the most famous of the grana-style cheeses. Parmigiano Reggiano is the original Parmesan cheese. For the cheese to be classified as Parmigiano Reggiano it must be made in certain areas of northern Italy, from cow's milk and under strictly controlled conditions. The words Parmigiano Reggiano are printed all over the rind of the hugh cheese wheels as proof of its authenticity.

Parmesan is best purchased fresh in a piece then grated as you require it. Once you have tried fresh Parmesan you will never bother with the grated powder that comes pre-packaged. The flavour of fresh Parmesan is much milder and the texture not as grainy.

QUARK

Sometimes called quarg, quark is one of the fresh unripened cheeses that have a clean, mild acid flavour and a spoonable consistency. If it is unavailable you can use creamed cottage cheese in its place.

RICOTTA

Traditionally made from the whey drained off during the production of mozzarella, ricotta is a snowy white cheese with a sweetish flavour and a moist texture. It is a cheese much loved by dieters for its low kilojoule (calorie) content. Ricotta is used extensively in cooking in dishes as diverse as cheesecakes and lasagne, however it is also delicious eaten on its own or with fruit.

Young Parmesan cheese is sweet and moist and is an excellent eating cheese. As the cheese ages the flavour becomes stronger and the texture drier. It is in this form that it is more commonly known and used.

STORING CHEESE

🍃 Always store cheese in the refrigerator. The refrigerator provides both low temperature and humidity – the best conditions for storing cheese.

🍃 To prevent cheese from drying out it is best to store it in its original wrapper. Once opened, wrap cheese in plastic food wrap or aluminium foil.

🍃 Allow cheese to come to room temperature before serving. As a general rule remove it from the refrigerator one hour prior to serving.

🍃 As a general guide, hard and semi-hard cheeses keep longer than curd and blue cheeses, which keep longer than fresh cheeses such as ricotta and mascarpone.

🍃 While freezing cheese is not recommended, matured and processed cheeses can be frozen. However their texture becomes crumbly and they can be slightly furry on the palate. Frozen cheese is best if it is thawed slowly in the refrigerator.

🍃 Due to the already crumbly texture of feta cheese it is not greatly affected by freezing.

CUTTING CHEESE

Cheese comes in many shapes and sizes and it is sometimes difficult to know how best to cut a large piece of cheese. This guide will assist you when next you are faced with large block of cheese.

Blocks: Cut in slices or cubes.

Large cylinders: Cut horizontally into thick slices, then into wedges.

Small cylinders: Cut into rounds.

Flat wheels: Cut into thin wedges.

Large wheels: Cut into wedges, then cut each wedge into chunks.

Balls: Cut into large wedges, then cut each wedge into small wedges.

Small rounds: Cut in half – this means that the cut surfaces can be pressed back together if all the cheese is not used.

Squares of soft cheese: Cut in half, then into thin strips.

Squares of hard, rinded cheese: Cut the square diagonally into four triangles, then each triangle into triangles. Cutting the cheese in this way gives each portion an equal amount of rind.

CHEESEBOARDS

🍂 The secret to a good cheeseboard is to offer a variety of decent-sized pieces of cheese. It is better to offer three or four good-sized pieces than eight or nine smaller portions. Not only will your cheeseboard look more attractive but also the cheese will retain flavour and freshness better.

🍂 A general guide is to allow at least 20 g/³/4 oz of each type of cheese per person.

🍂 For a basic cheeseboard or platter, offer a Cheddar, a blue cheese and a Camembert or Brie with plain crackers or crusty bread. You might also like to add some fresh fruit – apples, pears, grapes, fresh dates – or dried fruits and nuts, all of which go particularly well with cheese.

🍂 Ideally each cheese should have its own knife so that the individual flavour of each cheese is retained.

🍂 When determining what cheeses you are going to serve take into consideration the number of people you intend to feed. Obviously the larger the group the more variety you can have.

🍂 French people serve the cheeseboard after the salad (which has followed the main course) and before the dessert. This allows the last of the wine to be drunk with the cheese.

INDEX

UK COOKERY EDITOR
Katie Swallow

EDITORIAL
Food Editor: Rachel Blackmore
Editorial Assistant: Ella Martin
Editorial Coordinator: Margaret Kelly
Recipe Development: Sheryle Eastwood, Lucy Kelly, Donna Hay,
Anneka Mitchell, Penelope Peel, Belinda Warn, Loukie Werle
Credits: Recipes pages 4, 5 by Annette Grimsdale; pages 10, 69 by
Louise Steel; pages 41, 68 by Pat Alburey; pages 45, 46, 47 by Lorna
Rhodes; pages 50, 51, 52 by Steven Wheeler; page 72 by Gordon
Grimsdale; page 73 by June Budgen

COVER
Designer: Chrissie Lloyd
Photography: Laurie Evans
Home Economist: Jacqueline Clark
Styling: Lesley Richardson

PHOTOGRAPHY
Simon Butcher, Per Ericson, Paul Grater, Ray Joyce, Ashley
Mackevicius, Harm Mol, Yanto Noerianto, Andy Payne, Jon
Stewart, Warren Webb

STYLING
Wendy Berecry, Belinda Clayton, Rosemary De Santis, Carolyn
Fienberg, Jacqui Hing, Michelle Gorry

DESIGN AND PRODUCTION
Manager: Sheridan Carter
Layout: Lulu Dougherty
Finished Art: Stephen Joseph
Design: Frank Pithers

Published by J.B. Fairfax Press Pty Ltd
A.C.N. 003 738 430
Formatted by J.B. Fairfax Press Pty Ltd
Output by Adtype, Sydney
Printed by Toppan Printing Co, Singapore

Includes Index
1 86343 095 4 (pbk)
1 85391 292 1

Distributed by J.B. Fairfax Press Ltd
9 Trinity Centre, Park Farm Estate
Wellingborough, Northants
Ph: (0933) 402330 Fax: (0933) 402234

Patricia J. Stockham
Deans Cottage
Monkton, Nr. Honiton
East Devon EX14 9QQ
Tel: 01404-44207